S. Edward Warren

Elements of Plane and Solid Free-Hand Geometrical Drawing, with Lettering

And some elements of geometrical ornamental design, including the principals of harmonic angular ratios, etc. In three parts.

S. Edward Warren

Elements of Plane and Solid Free-Hand Geometrical Drawing, with Lettering
And some elements of geometrical ornamental design, including the principals of harmonic angular ratios, etc. In three parts.

ISBN/EAN: 9783337286095

Printed in Europe, USA, Canada, Australia, Japan

Cover: Foto ©Paul-Georg Meister /pixelio.de

More available books at **www.hansebooks.com**

INDUSTRIAL SCIENCE DRAWING.

ELEMENTS OF PLANE AND SOLID

FREE-HAND GEOMETRICAL

DRAWING,

WITH

LETTERING;

AND SOME ELEMENTS OF

GEOMETRICAL ORNAMENTAL DESIGN,

INCLUDING THE PRINCIPLES OF HARMONIC ANGULAR RATIOS, ETC.

IN THREE PARTS:

PART I.—PLANE DRAWING, OR FROM "THE FLAT."
PART II.—SOLID DRAWING, OR FROM "THE ROUND."
PART III.—ELEMENTS OF GEOMETRIC BEAUTY.

FOR DRAUGHTSMEN AND ARTISANS; AND TEACHERS AND STUDENTS OF INDUSTRIAL AND MECHANICAL DRAWING.

BY

S. EDWARD WARREN, C.E.,

FORMER PROFESSOR IN THE RENSSELAER POLYTECHNIC INSTITUTE, AND MASS. INST. OF TECHNOLOGY; AND BOSTON NORMAL ART SCHOOL; AND AUTHOR OF A COMPLETE SERIES OF TEXT-BOOKS ON DESCRIPTIVE GEOMETRY AND INSTRUMENTAL DRAWING.

NEW YORK:
JOHN WILEY & SONS,
15 ASTOR PLACE,
1878

COPYRIGHT,
WILEY & SONS.
1878.

Trow's
Printing and Bookbinding Co.,
205-213 *East 12th St.*,
NEW YORK.

CONTENTS.

	PAGE
PREFACE..	VII
PREFACE TO THE SECOND EDITION...............................	XI

PART I.

PLANE DRAWING.

CHAPTER I.

Exercises on directions of straight lines............................	1
First principles..	1
Materials..	2
Directions...	2
Single lines...	3
Parallels..	5
Opposite lines..	5
Double lines..	6
Use of the copy-book. Size of figures	6

CHAPTER II.

Elementary and practical exercises on right angles................	7
Principles..	7
Examples of single lines at right angles, with sides horizontal and vertical	8
With sides oblique..	9

	PAGE
Right angles	9
Pairs of parallels at right angles. The pairs horizontal and vertical	10
The pairs in oblique positions	10
Practical examples	10
Occasions for free-hand sketching	11

CHAPTER III.

Distances, and division of straight lines	12
Principles	12
Exercises in marking off a given distance	12
Division of lines into equal parts	14
Practical applications	15
Enlargement and reduction	18

CHAPTER IV.

Circles and their division	20
Principles	20
Examples. Circles and Arcs	20
Division of circles	22

CHAPTER V.

Proportional angles	23
Principles	23
Elementary examples	24
Practical examples	26

CHAPTER VI.

Figures bounded by straight lines	27
Principles	27
Elementary examples	28
Practical examples	31

CHAPTER VII.

Rectilinear and circular combinations	33
Principles	33
Exercises	34

CHAPTER VIII.

Curves, and curved objects in general. Ex. (103–118)............ 37

CHAPTER IX.

Lettering... 47
General principles.. 47
Roman capitals.. 48
Letters in general. Their classification and construction......... 51
Practical remarks... 54

PART II.

SOLID DRAWING.

CHAPTER I.

Object, or model drawing. Rectilinear models...................... 57
Definitions and principles... 57
Exercises... 59
Curvilinear models.. 60

CHAPTER II.

Perspective and projection free-hand drawing...................... 62
Definitions... 62
Indicated exercises. Properties and treatment of wood............. 63

CHAPTER III.

Pictorial projection sketching..................................... 66
Definitions and principles... 66
Isometrical drawings... 66
Practical applications.. 68

PART III.

ELEMENTS OF GEOMETRIC BEAUTY.

CHAPTER I.

Elementary ideas. Unity, Variety, Freedom........................ 73

CHAPTER II.

Numerical and geometrical expression of the elementary ideas.......... 78

CHAPTER III.

General applications of the idea of beauty in ratios. Analogy of form and sound... 84

CHAPTER IV.

Application to triangles and rectangles................................ 90
Triangles.. 90
Rectangles... 93

CHAPTER V.

Geometric beauty of polygons. Geometrical design.................... 96

CHAPTER VI.

Curvilinear geometric beauty. Circles and ellipses.................... 102

CHAPTER VII.

Curvilinear geometric beauty. Ovals................................ 110
Natural and artificial curves... 110
The egg-form, or oval.. 111
Industrial applications 120
The method by co-ordinates.. 123

CHAPTER VIII.

Geometric symbolism... 126
Definitions and general illustrations.................................. 126
Geometric illustrations.. 127

FROM THE ORIGINAL PREFACE.

In geometrical, or mechanical drawing, exclusive reliance for accuracy may, in theory, be placed on good drawing instruments, properly used.

Practically, these instruments are not absolutely perfect as means to the ends to be accomplished by them, and from this, and momentary negligences of the draftsman, they are not infallible in accuracy of operation.

But, viewing the eye and hand simply as instruments for executing conceptions of form, they are incomparably more perfect and varied in their capacities in this respect than drafting instruments; and well directed practice should, and will, bring out this capacity.

Hence, other things being the same, he will be the most expert and elegant draftsman, whose eye is most reliable in its estimates of form and size, and whose free hand is most skilled in expressing these elements of figure.

Accordingly, in harmony with the law of easy gradations and connecting links which pervades nature, we find a special branch of free drawing which is peculiarly well adapted for a preliminary training of the eye and hand of the geometrical draftsman. This training consists simply in drawing various single and combined geometrical lines and figures, of various forms and sizes, by the unassisted hand; and constitutes a connecting link between ornamental free drawing and instrumental drawing.

These brief reflections have resulted from a recent inspection of a few simple pencil plates of such drawings forgotten for a long time, having been made by the writer several years since, in connection with the conduct of a short course of exercises of the kind above described.

As a further, and I hope not useless fruit of the foregoing views, the following little course is presented to all who, as draftsmen, may promise themselves benefit from the use of it, and for exercises of mingled interrogation and practice in preparatory and industrial schools.

By means of a love of skill and accuracy in the use of eye and hand, exercises like those of this volume may be made a pastime for the improving (especially if social) enlivenment of numerous odd moments, those times when *many subordinate excellencies can be acquired or perpetuated without interference with one's larger industries.*

Writing, as merely auxiliary to daily business, is not, in its intention, a branch of drawing. But, as an ornamental art, it is a species of free-hand drawing, not geometrical, however. Hence I have not treated of writing, while ample instructions on lettering have been deemed a due portion of the contents of this volume, since, moreover, the usual small size of letters makes their construction by hand alone more convenient than by the use of drafting instruments.

The good tendencies of accurate drawing in regard to mind and character are worthy of notice. Practice in such drawing directly tends to make *close* and *accurate* observers, who will thus gain *distinct conceptions* of the objects of attention, and so of thought generally, and who will then more readily pass on to *fidelity in the representation* of their observations and conceptions.

NEWTON, Mass., *January*, 1873.

NEW PREFACE.

In distinguishing between artists proper; and those engaged in the study or practice of *industrial design*—that of various wares and fabrics—together with those engaged in *engineering and mechanical study or practice,* including instrumental drawing; it seems appropriate that both the latter classes should receive a special training—useful also to all—in the *free-hand drawing of regular forms.* Hence my former small work was put forth, partly as an experiment. Increasing interest in the subject, and the measure of favor accorded to that less complete volume, has induced the author to studiously revise, remodel, and enlarge his work, adding many new figures, mostly on plates.

Of the three PARTS, into which the present volume is divided, PART II. is largely, and PART III., almost wholly new.

PART III. may interest the general reader. It contains, apparently the most appropriate principal extension of the volume, a concise presentation of the elements of geometric beauty, based, in general, on the ingenious and presumably correct theory of D. R. Hay; but containing principles and applications not found in his "Principles of Symmetric Beauty." Especially, the ovals, or egg-forms, derived naturally, and in unlimited variety, are believed to be new, and an improvement upon his "composite ellipse."

The subject of symbolism may, in some aspects, of course, be turned into pleasantry. Still, as its use has prevailed for centuries in some departments, there seems to be no reason for not extending it to others. I have sought to simplify, and to improve as much as possible, the very little that room could be found for, on this subject.

The figures or patterns in this volume may have a threefold use: *First*, merely as copies for imitation, in acquiring skill of eye and hand. *Second*, as standards, from which to make as many *variations* by recombination of elements, as ingenuity can invent. *Third*, as objects to which to apply the principles of beauty developed in Part III. Bearing this in mind, it will be seen, that the appropriate range of use of this volume may extend through Public and Private Preparatory Schools, Artizan's and other Evening Schools; Schools of Design, and the earlier classes in Polytechnic Schools.

The pupil's figures may conveniently be drawn in blank copybooks, easily procurable, and, in most cases should be considerably larger than the copies, in order to cultivate a broader freedom of movement of the hand.

By a new process, enabling the plates to be close imitations of the autograph originals, the rigid straitness of ruled lines, which could not well be imitated by the free-hand, is avoided; and the copies are such as the pains-taking pupil may reasonably be expected to equal, and encouraged to excel.

Grateful for the favor long accorded to his other elementary works, the author, ever bearing in mind, and recommending joint attention to *principles* and *practice*, hopes to make them still more acceptable by extending the work of thorough revision (for the first time, excepting the Projection Drawing) to all of them.

NEWTON, Mass., *August*, 1878.

FREE-HAND GEOMETRICAL DRAWING.

PART I.

PLANE DRAWING.

CHAPTER I.

EXERCISES ON DIRECTIONS OF STRAIGHT LINES.

First Principles.

The direction of a straight line is its invariable tendency towards some fixed point.

The directions of two lines may be alike. The lines are then said to have the same direction, and are called *parallel*.

The drawing of *parallel lines*, or those whose *directions are alike*, is simpler than that of lines whose *directions are different*, and hence is here considered first.

A line which is "straight up and down," or perpendicular to the surface of water, like this, when the book is held upright, is called *vertical*.
A *level* line is called *horizontal*.

The force of gravity acts vertically, hence objects rest with most stability in a vertical position on horizontal surfaces. Likewise, man himself, naturally stands upright, or *vertically*, and, generally, on surfaces whose lines are level, or horizontal. Hence vertical and horizontal are the simplest, most familiar, or primitive directions of lines, and will be first considered.

Lines which are neither vertical nor horizontal, are *oblique*. Also lines lying in any flat surface, and not representing either of these positions, are called oblique.

Before commencing the succeeding exercises, the learner should be provided with the following materials; and, throughout his progress, should carefully follow the subjoined general directions.

Materials.

For the practice of quite young pupils, where substantial accuracy, rather than fineness of execution is expected, quite cheap paper, or even a slate and pencil will answer.

For other pupils, blank drawing books of the usual form, everywhere easily obtained, may be used ; or, drawing paper may be cut into plates of convenient size, and kept in a paper-case such as any one can make for himself.

A common semi-circular "*protractor*," a semi-circular piece of thin material, divided into degrees on its curved edge.

A ruler 10 inches long and 1 inch wide.

Moderately soft pencils, as Faber's No. 2 and 3.

Prepared india rubber, free from grit, of the best kind now known as " Artist's gum."

Spare pieces of paper, one, on which to rest the hand and so protect the drawing, and another on which to try the pencils. Also a strip for a measure of distances.

A fine file, on which the pencil can, by a rolling rubbing motion, be most neatly and readily sharpened to a round point.

When accuracy on a large scale is sought, as a training for bold sketching, plates, 10 ins. by 14 ins. of buff manilla drafting paper, and crayons, should be substituted for pencils, and small plates and figures. In fact, this may be done as a preliminary counterpoise to the somewhat cramping tendency of the mostly minute accuracy required in mechanical drawing. But for direct training in this accuracy, the pencils, and small plates, should be used as above indicated.

Directions.

Depend on the unassisted eye and hand alone, from the beginning. They will, in due time, amply reward the reliance placed upon them. Ruler, Protractor, and Measure may be used to *test* the *straightness*, *direction* and *length* of lines already drawn, so that if incorrect they can be re-drawn. But they should never be used to locate, limit, or rule the lines; for thus no education is afforded to the eye and hand, only trifling skill is gained by them, and so the main object of the exercises is missed.

If a line is found incorrect, first consider carefully how it differs from what it was meant to be, then erase it, and study its direction well, and try again. *Excellent quality*, and not great quantity of drawing, is to be the chief object of ambition.

Avoid the use of the rubber by studying well the position and lengths of the lines *before* drawing them. *Mean* to have them appear in a certain way, and then make them so, as truly as possible; rather than hastily make a careless sketch and then seek how to correct it.

Be sure that a figure is as well done as possible at the time, in obedience to the preceding rules, before attempting a new figure.

Hold the pencil between the thumb and forefinger, and resting on the tip of the second finger. It can then be moved both with freedom and steadiness.

In drawing lines towards or from you, let the elbow be at some distance from the body. In drawing lines from side to side let the elbow be close to the body.

Arrange the seat and paper so as to look at the paper in a direction at right angles to it, without stooping, and let the desk be low enough not to interfere with the elbows.

Though all the lines of the following figures are horizontal, when the book lies flat, yet, for the sake of brevity, it may be understood that all those lines shall be *called vertical*, which are so when the book is held vertically. Lines from side to side may be *called horizontal*, and others, *oblique*.

Remember especially to sketch each of the figures, first in very faint lines, which can easily be erased if incorrect, before drawing the firm heavy lines of the finished figures. Do not, however creep along the line by short, disconnected, and hesitating steps, thus, —— `—` —— `—` ,— — but mark the line by a firm and unbroken movement, first lightly, thus, ——————————————————— and then heavily, thus: ———————————————————.

Single Lines.

EXAMPLE, 1. Draw *vertical* lines, beginning at *the top*, and far enough apart to prevent each from being a guide to the other, as a parallel. Thus let these lines be drawn at the middle and ends of the upper half of the plate. See A, Pl. I.

Ex. 2. The same on the lower half of the plate, but beginning the lines at *the bottom*. See Pl. I.

Ex. 3. Mark two points so as to be connected by a vertical line, and then draw a line joining them, beginning a little *above* the *upper point.*

Ex. 4. The same, but beginning *below* the *lower point.*

These, and all the examples, should be varied, by taking lines of various lengths.

Ex. 5. Draw horizontal lines, beginning at the left, and far apart, as at the top, middle and bottom of the left hand half of a plate. See Pl. I.

Ex. 6. The same on the right hand half of the plate, and beginning at the right. This will require special care.

Ex. 7. Mark two points so as to join them by a horizontal line, beginning to the left of the left hand one, and draw to the right.

Ex. 8. The same, only begin to the right of the right hand one.

The foregoing constructions not all shown on Pl. I. will divide the plate into quarters, in which the following may be drawn.

Ex. 9 to 12. May consist of the four preceding variations in the manner of drawing, applied to an oblique line, which inclines *from* the body and to the *right,* thus:

Ex. 13 to 16. May consist of four similar constructions of lines which incline *from* the body but to the left.

The last two examples should also be practised with the two following variations: First, let the lines be *more nearly vertical* than horizontal, thus:

DIRECTIONS OF STRAIGHT LINES. 5

Second, let them be *more nearly horizontal* than vertical, thus:

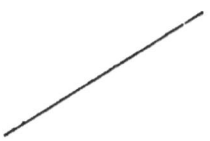

Parallels.

The following Examples permit so many variations in the order of construction, that each one, as numbered, must be generally understood to include several particular varieties.

Ex. 17. Draw *two* vertical parallels, first drawing the left hand one first; and second, the right hand one first. Also draw each, in the four ways described in Examples 1 to 4.

Ex. 18. Likewise draw *two* horizontal parallels, first, drawing the upper one first; and second, the lower one first, and each as in examples 5 to 8.

Ex. 19. Draw *several* vertical parallels, beginning alternately at top and bottom. See *a.*, Pl. I.

Ex. 20 to 22. May consist of similar variations in drawing two or more horizontal parallels. See *b.*, Pl. I.

Ex. 23 to 28. May consist of similar exercises on two or more oblique parallels situated as in examples 9 to 16, and including the variations in the amount of obliquity there pointed out.

Opposite Lines.

These are lines starting at a given point; and proceeding in opposite directions, thus:

or towards each other from their outer extremities.

Ex. 29. Draw opposite lines, one upwards, and one downwards from the given point.

Ex. 30. Do., one to the right, and one to the left of a given point.

Ex. 31. Do., in the principal varieties of oblique position.

Ex. 32. Is a comprehensive one, consisting of the variation of the three preceding, by beginning to draw the opposite lines in each case from their outer extremities.

Double Lines.

All the preceding examples may be made in double lines; that is, lines as close together as they can be made without touching, and at first of the *same size*, and then, of *different* sizes.

Useful practice under this head consists in filling various figures, such as triangles, squares, polygons and circles, with parallel lines, which should be made equidistant by the eye.

General Example. Construct a series of examples of figures thus filled, each with one, two, three, or four sets of parallels; which will form an elegant imitation of bold line engraving. See Pl. I., Fig. 1.

Use of the Copy-book—Size of Figures.

The figures, many of which are, for convenience, printed of small size, and with the text where they are described, should be considerably enlarged as drawn in the copy-book, by the pupil.

The plates give a better idea of the size and style of the figures as they should be drawn. Only, as the pupil's plates may be more numerous and less crowded, his figures may be larger at pleasure, making from one to six to a plate, according to their character.

Indeed, where the figures are done with crayons, they should be made much larger, and may each be made to fill a buff manilla paper plate twice as large as those of the copy-book. Plates IX. and X. contain such figures; and when so drawn, they cultivate a greater freedom of movement of the hand, combined with exactness, than is secured by the finer work with the pencil alone.

To avoid injurious wear of the copy-book by repeated trials, it may often be best to draw the figures first on loose waste plates.

CHAPTER II.

ELEMENTARY AND PRACTICAL EXERCISES ON RIGHT ANGLES.

Principles.

BEAUTY of form, considered as residing in certain geometrical properties of regular figures, results from certain proportions between their parts. These proportions may be regarded as arising from the *relative lengths* of the distinguishing *lines* of the objects; or from the *relative sizes* of their *angles*.

In moving, whether to walk, or to merely draw a line, we must begin each movement at a given point. The *direction* of our movement is first in our thoughts, rather than its *extent*. We first, if not oftenest, think, or ask, "*which way*" than "*how far.*" *Direction* is therefore a more primary idea than *length*. An *angle*, however, is merely difference between directions from a certain point. Hence *angular proportions*, or the proportion between the *angles* of a figure, are more elementary than *linear proportions*, or those between the *lengths of the lines* of the figure, and will be first considered.

In doing this it will be convenient to find first some angle as a *natural standard of comparison* for all others, and this we now proceed to do. When, then, two lines are so situated that, in moving on one of them, we do not at all move in the direction of the other, their directions are said to be *independent*.

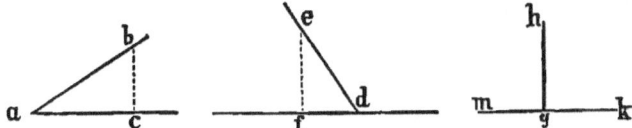

Thus, in these figures, by going from *a* to *b*, we find ourselves at the distance *ac* to the right of *a*. So by moving from *d* to *e* we go a distance equal to *df* in the direction of the line *df*. But, *when the two angles formed by the meeting lines are equal*, as at *mgh* and *kgh*, we do not, in moving to any distance on *gh*, progress at all to the right or left of *gh*. Hence the directions of *gh* and *mk* are *independent*, and the angle included between them is the *natural* standard with which to compare all other angles. This angle between *independent directions* is called a *right angle ;* and now some of the subsequent exercises are to consist in constructing, by the eye, various proportional parts of a right angle.

But, again, it follows from the explanation of vertical and horizontal directions, in Chapter I., that a right angle is in its simplest, most natural, or *standard position,* when its sides are in the *fundamental directions* of *vertical* and *horizontal.* We therefore begin with right angles in this position. Observe first, however, that we do not say perpendicular and horizontal, but *vertical* and horizontal, for a line in any position whatever, is perpendicular to another when it is at right angles with it, but there is but *one vertical,* or "straight up and down" direction.

Examples of Single Lines at Right Angles, with Sides Horizontal and Vertical.

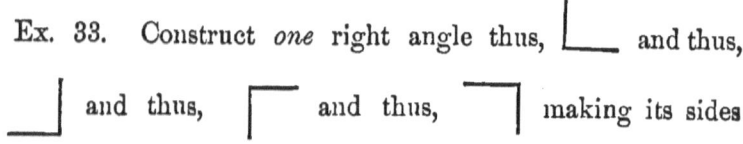

Ex. 33. Construct *one* right angle thus, and thus, and thus, and thus, making its sides from one to three inches in length, *each side ending at its intersection with the other.* Slight additions will give these simple elementary figures a pleasing character as designs for geometrical borders and corner pieces, thus :

designs which it is easy to make evenly by observing the direction to pencil each line faintly at first, while locating it as intended.

Observing that the beauty of a border depends upon its *expressiveness,* as an echo of some characteristic of the work which it encloses, the first design would make an agreeable corner, for a plate of figures made up of points and straight lines. The second, with its swelled lines, suggests *strength* in the corner of the border; which can also be gained by a diagonal from the outer corner to, or a little beyond the inner corner.

Ex. 34. Construct *two* right angles, by prolonging one of the sides beyond the vertex of the angle, thus, ⊥ and thus, ⊢ and thus, ⊤ and thus, ⊣

making the sides of each angle from two to four inches long, in this and the following figures.

Ex. 35. Construct *four* right angles, by prolonging each side through its point of intersection with the other, thus ─┼─

Right Angles with sides Oblique.

Ex. 36. Repeat Ex. 33 with the sides in various oblique positions, and of various lengths, thus:

Ex. 37. In like manner, repeat Ex. 34, thus:

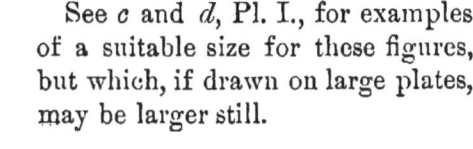

Ex. 38. Similarly, repeat Ex. 35, thus, but in each case make the lines from one to three or four inches long, from the point of intersection.

See *c* and *d*, Pl. I., for examples of a suitable size for these figures, but which, if drawn on large plates, may be larger still.

PAIRS OF PARALLELS AT RIGHT ANGLES.

The Pairs Horizontal and Vertical.

Many variations can be made, and should be, in the order of drawing each of the following figures. Thus the vertical lines can both be begun at top or bottom, or one in each way; also, the horizontal lines may both be begun at the left end, or right end, or one in each way. Again, both of the vertical lines may be drawn first, or both of the horizontal ones, or one of each in succession.

Ex. 39. To give a more ornamental character to these simple elements, after seeking *truth* of representation, only, in the preceding elementary figures, they may consist in combinations of faint and heavy lines, as shown in a part of the following figures, all of which should be made of lines from a half inch to three or more inches long.

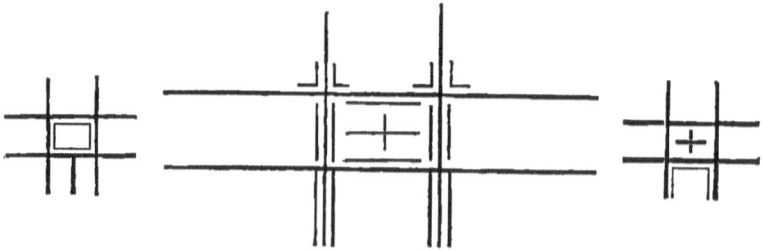

The pairs in oblique positions.

Ex. 40. Repeat Ex. 39, as follows :

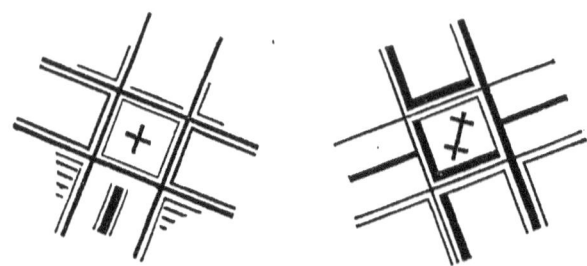

Practical Examples.

Ex. 41. The preceding elementary examples afford all the operations necessary in forming many simple drawings, either of geometrical designs for *surface ornament*, or of objects.

EXERCISES ON RIGHT ANGLES. 11

A specimen or two of each is added in this example.

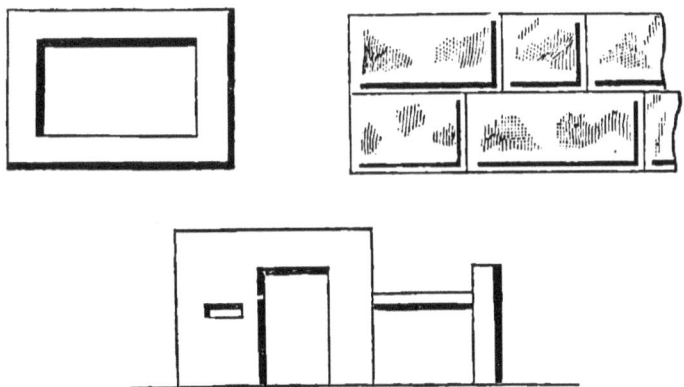

The pupil is here again reminded always to make his figures very much larger than those of the book, making *from two to four* on a plate like those here shown.

Ex. 42. Figs. 2, 3, 4, Pl. I., exhibit other practical examples of constructions containing only lines at right angles to each other.

Occasions for Free-hand Sketching.

The travelling student, architect, engineer, mason or builder may often find it desirable to make hasty sketches of neatly contrived details or structures, whether in masonry, wood, or metal. So also may persons of any and all occupations, when seeking to "give an idea" of something which they wish to have constructed; and, in both cases, drafting instruments and time to use them may not be at command.

The examples mentioned, and many similar ones which they may suggest, or which may usefully be collected by observation, should therefore be carefully drawn on various scales by the pupil, as a means of acquiring skill in the useful accomplishment of *readily* making free-hand sketches of *geometrical industrial objects*.

CHAPTER III.

DISTANCES, AND DIVISION OF STRAIGHT LINES.

Principles.

HAVING considered various *directions* of straight lines, we are prepared to estimate and represent *various distances* upon them.

Distances are *equal* or *unequal*. When unequal, we often wish to *compare* them. Distances may be compared, *first*, by taking one from the other, and thus finding their *difference*. This shows *how much* greater, or smaller, one distance is than the other.

Distances may also be compared, *second*, by observing how many times one is contained in the other, and thus finding their *ratio*. This shows *how many times* greater the larger distance is than the smaller, or *what part* the smaller is of the greater.

When we compare lines in this second way, we speak of them as *proportional*, or as *being in proportion* to each other, or as *having a certain proportion* to each other.

An indefinite line is one that has no given limits. In representing distances, we may either mark *a given distance* several successive times on an indefinite line; or, we may divide a given line into equal parts, and so *find* a series of equal distances.

Exercises in Marking off a Given Distance.

Ex. 43. Draw straight lines in different directions, and mark by the eye, the same distance, once, on all of them, thus:

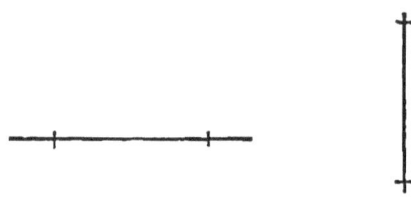

DISTANCES AND DIVISION OF STRAIGHT LINES. 13

Transfer the distance on the first line to the edge of a slip of paper, and with this, as a measure, see if the distances on the other lines all agree with this measure. If not, observe whether they are too large or too small, and then, without making any mark on the paper before removing the measure, take away the measure, and correct the distances by the eye.

Ex. 44. In like manner, mark a given distance several times, on lines in various directions; thus:

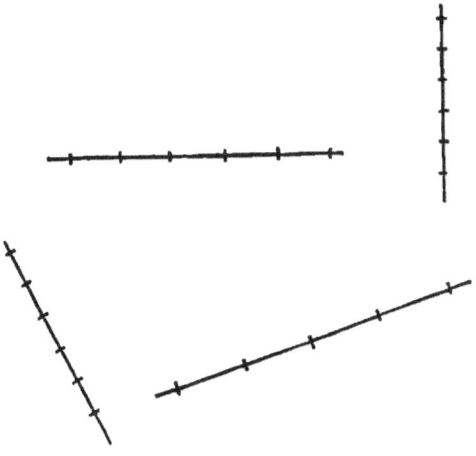

Ex. 45. Draw lines in several directions through the same point, and mark equal distances from the point on all of them; thus:

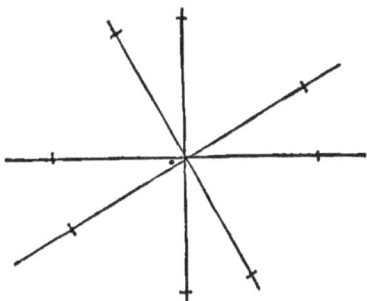

Division of Lines into Equal Parts.

Ex. 46. Divide lines in various positions, as shown below, into two equal parts. This is done by marking the middle point of the line, and is called *bisecting* the line. Then apply the paper measure, and see if the two parts are equal. If they are not, the error found at the end of the line will be double the error in the required half. If three parts had been required, this final error would have been three times the error in the single third of the line, and so on. Then make the necessary corrections, accordingly.

To distinguish these figures from the preceding, mark only the *ends* of the line by dashes extending across the line.

Ex. 47. Divide a line into four equal parts. To do this, bisect the whole line, and then bisect each of its halves.

In each of these exercises, let the given line be taken in various positions, though but one may be shown in the book.

In like manner, that is, by bisecting each quarter of a line, we should obtain eight equal parts, etc.

Ex. 48. To divide a line into three equal parts, that is, to *trisect* it. Estimate one-third of the line, and bisect the remainder.

To divide a line into nine equal parts, divide each of its thirds into three equal parts.

Ex. 49. In the preceding examples, we have divided each of the larger spaces into the same number of parts into which the whole was first divided.

Let a line now be divided into *six* equal parts, for example. Half of a line is more easily estimated than a third, hence divide the line first into halves. Also, having done this, one-third of a short distance, as the half line, is more easily estimated than a third of the longer whole line, hence divide each half into thirds, giving six equal parts in the whole line.

Ex. 50. To divide a line into any prime number, as five, seven, eleven, etc., of equal parts, it is necessary to estimate at once the fifth, seventh, eleventh, etc., part of the whole line. Yet this may be done more readily by dividing the line into two or more parts. Thus, one *third* of a line to be divided into *seven* equal parts would contain two and one-third of those parts, and thus we could more easily estimate the size of one of those parts.

Practical Applications.

Pl. II. gives examples of various useful exercises in *distance, direction, division.*

In order to enter upon the drawing of these figures, and many similar ones, with proper ideas and spirit, it is necessary to understand that, although they would, in final and finished practice, be drawn with instruments, yet it is highly useful to draw them also first by the eye, and for various reasons, such as follow.

First ; it may (see p. 11) often be desirable to make rapid sketches, when instruments are not at hand. *Second ;* instruments are liable to be displaced unconsciously to the draftsmen, giving unequal spaces, if dividers are jarred, or a scale mistakenly used; and untrue directions, if a ruler be displaced. In these cases, the eye may be so accurately trained as to readily detect errors, which if long undiscovered would, and do, occasion great annoyance. *Third ;* the eye so trained will often enable the draftsman to make small and simple divisions, especially those requiring only repeated bisection, as *halves, fourths,* etc., as readily and perfectly by the eye, as with the compasses.

All the following figures were originally drawn strictly as here directed, the divisions being tested by marking them on the edge of a slip of paper, and the directions, see especially the diagonals in Fig. 6, by tracing them at first very faintly.

The pupil should therefore begin with an effectual ambition and purpose to perfect his work without instruments.

Ex. 51. *Customary black-board exercises.*—Besides figures drawn on the black-board only for varied practice, or some other special purpose, various common subjects of study customarily require the drawing of numerous black-board diagrams. It should never be supposed, that because these diagrams are temporary, they may be carelessly drawn. On the contrary, on the teacher's part, neat diagrams lend interest to explanations, and naturally stimulate the learner to draw equally good ones; while on the pupil's part, the pains taken in making them helps to form the invaluable habit of doing as well as possible whatever one does.

Accordingly, Fig. 1 is a diagram, connected with the use of instruments, and Fig. 2, is from plane geometry.

Fig. 1 represents what is called a diagonal scale, from its diagonal lines at 1, 2, 3. A scale is a contrivance for representing any actual measure, as a foot, yard, or mile, by some other measure, usually a smaller one. Thus, let the distance from 0, to 1yd., be *two inches*, but let it represent one yard. It will then be called one yard. The next lower denomination is feet, hence, making the distance 0, 3ft. equal to two inches divide it into three equal parts, each of which will therefore represent a foot, and will be called a foot. Now suppose we wish to represent fourths of a foot, or three-inch spaces. Draw five equi-distant parallel lines, at any convenient distance apart, as shown, and divide the distance 0', 3' on the lowest line, into three equal parts, and draw the diagonals as shown. Then you see that as $0'a$ is one fourth of $0'0$; ac is one fourth of 01. But 01 is one foot, hence ac is one fourth of one foot or three inches.

In like manner, the distance between the two heavy dots is 1 yard, 1 ft., and nr, which is three-fourths of 01, or 9 inches.

As a drawing-exercise, the points to be observed are to make those lines straight and parallel, and those divisions equal, that are intended to be so.

The pupil can exercise his ingenuity in making other diagonal scales from the full description given of this one; as, for example, one of feet, inches, and half-inches; or one of units, 10ths, and 100ths.

In Fig. 2, the exercise consists in making ab perfectly parallel to AB, and cd to AD; and in drawing Ab straight from A to b and Ad, from A to d. Then, triangles, like AaB, and AbB, having the same base, AB, and equal altitudes (the perpendicular distance between ab and AB) have equal areas. Also, as the like is true of the triangles AcD, and AdD, the triangle Abd is equivalent to the polygon AaBDc.

Ex. 52. *Floor and wall decoration.*—Pl. II., Figs. 3, 4, and 5, are examples requiring equal divisions of one or more sizes, and parallel lines in different directions.

Fig. 3, represents diagonal floor-work in two woods, the construction being founded upon the square 0, 6, 6, S. Divide the sides of this square into any desired *even* number of equal parts, and draw Sd and the parallels to it through the corners and middle points of the sides of the square to form the *parallel bands* of flooring; each band being filled with narrow diagonal strips. These strips are drawn parallel to the sides of the square, through points of division on an adjacent side; as py, parallel to 6, 6, through 5 on 0, 6.

Finally, the two woods may be arranged in two ways; *first*, touching each other on a common edge, as at ab; *second*, touching only at the corners, as at c and d.

Fig. 4, represents a toothed cornice, the shaded portions giving the effect of shadows.

Fig. 5, represents an ornamental band of triangular points, the darker portions indicating a darker color. In dividing, equally, the top and bottom lines, be careful to make the points, as a, of the triangles exactly over the middle points, as b, of their bases.

Ex. 53. Fig. 6, gives further occasion for practice in *combined equal division;* in the equal bars, and in the larger equal spaces between them. Also in the *direction* of the diagonal brace.

In this, and all similar cases, the *divisions*, first made only by the eye (p. 2, Directions), may be adjusted by the aid of a slip of paper to the edge of which a division of each kind can be transferred and used to test the others.

The *directions* are adjusted by sketching them very faintly, just skimming the point of the pencil along the paper, until they are found to be correct, when the faint traces thus obtained can be firmly drawn in heavier lines with a softer pencil.

Enlargement and Reduction.

Pl. II., Figs. 7 and 8, and Fig. 9, exhibit two methods of accomplishing an often desirable and useful purpose, that of reducing a given figure in any desired ratio. One of these may be called the method by *subdivision,* the other, that by *concentration.*

Ex. 54. Fig. 7, may represent a frame in the form of a capital "A," carrying a plummet, and standing in a window opening of irregular outline. Fig. 8 is a reduced copy in which each side of the auxiliary enclosing square is five-eighths of that in Fig. 7. By subdivision of this square into the same number of smaller squares in each figure, the portion of the figure embraced in each small square will be so small that it can be very accurately drawn by the eye.

This method may be applied to the sketching of large objects, by substituting for the subdivided square of Fig. 7, a frame of equidistant threads, crossing each other so as to form squares. Then by setting this frame in some suitable fixed position, and viewing the given object through it, from some fixed point, the portion of the object seen in each thread square can be traced in the corresponding compartment of the similarly subdivided square on the paper.

When, however, the ability already exists to draw objects accurately from the original, this method by the thread frame is *unnecessary.* And where the purpose is to acquire this ability by a sufficiently extended practice in sketching from original objects, the same method might only hinder the result. But in the many cases still remaining, the method will be found useful.*

Ex. 55. Fig. 9, represents a given irregular figure, the outer one, reduced to the smaller one by means of the auxiliary lines which converge from its angles to 0. The truth of the method will be apparent by conceiving 0 to be the vertex of a pyramid whose base is the given figure, and the reduced figure to be a section of this pyramid, parallel to its base. Each side of the

---

* See my *E'ementary* PERSPECTIVE, PART II., Chap. IV.

smaller figure will then be parallel to the corresponding side of the larger one, and all of the converging lines will be divided in the same manner. That is, if any one of them be bisected, as in the figure, all of them will be bisected. Thus the method, when executed by the free hand throughout, affords practice in three things, *first*, the drawing of straight lines in various directions, each joining two given points; *second*, in drawing parallel lines; *third*, in the equal division of lines.

Pupils can profitably practice extensively on these two methods of copying, with variation of size. The former conveniently applies to the copying of geographical maps, carpet, paper, and inlaid patterns of regular form, and to letters. The latter method applies better to polygons, regular or irregular, as the boundaries of the map of a field.

CHAPTER IV.

CIRCLES AND THEIR DIVISION.

Principles.

DIRECTION is, as before said, tendency towards a certain point A straight line has but one direction at all of its points.

A curve constantly changes its direction.

The simplest curve, and the one which will be the natural standard of comparison for all other curves, is the one which changes its direction at a uniform rate. The *circle* is such a curve, and all its points are at equal distances from one point within called its centre. The circle is, therefore, the simplest curve, and standard of comparison for other curves.

Examples. Circles and Arcs.

Ex. 56. To draw a circle. Sketch, faintly, several lines through a point, taken as the centre of the circle, and, from this point, mark off equal distances on each of these lines. Then through the points thus given draw the circle, thus:

Ex. 57. To draw the circle without drawing the lines through its centre. With the paper measure, mark a number of points all at the same distance from the centre, and then sketch the circle through those points.

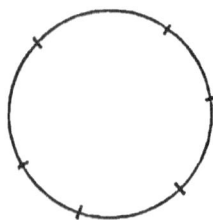

In both of these constructions, use fewer and fewer guides, and at last sketch a circle with no guiding point but its centre. Also practice often in rapidly drawing circles by hand on the black board.

The distance from the centre to the circumference of a circle, is called its radius. The distance across the circle, through its centre is its diameter.

Parallel circles have the same centre, and are called *concentric*. A portion of the circumference of a circle, is called an arc.

Ex. 58. Draw circular arcs in various positions, and of various radii, and length, thus:

Ex. 59. Draw parallel arcs and circles, of various radii, and the former also of various lengths and in various positions, thus ; and then *mark their centres.*

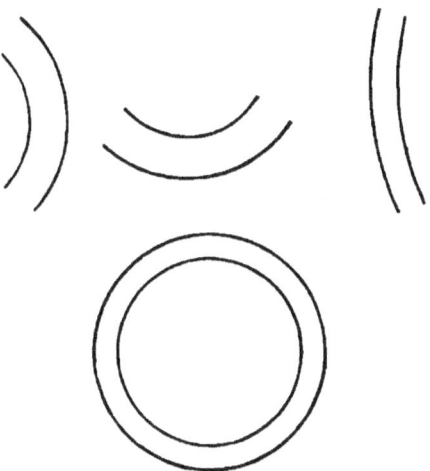

Division of Circles.

Circles, or arcs, may, like straight lines, have given distances marked off upon them, and may be divided into equal parts.

The line which joins the extremities of an arc, is called the chord of that arc. When the arc is very short, its length cannot be ordinarily distinguished from that of its chord. It is on this principle that any given straight distance may be transferred to a circle or to any curve.

Ex. 60. To lay off a given distance on a circle or arc, divide that distance into a sufficient number of small equal parts, and then mark off on the circle, or arc, the same number of similar equal parts, thus, where the straight line is the given distance.

Ex. 61. Any diameter of a circle divides it into two equal parts, therefore draw several circles, and one diameter in each; but in different positions in the different circles, which may also be of various sizes.

Ex. 62. Two diameters at right angles to each other, divide a circle into four equal parts. Draw such diameters in various positions.

Ex. 63. The radius of a circle applies just six times to its circumference. Then lay off the radius once, as a chord of the circumference, as explained above, and then mark the other divisions, equal to the one thus obtained.

Ex. 64. Bisect each quarter circle in Ex. 62, which will give eight equal parts in the whole circle.

This bisection can then be continued to any extent, giving sixteenths, etc., of the circumference.

Ex. 65. Continue these exercises by trisecting the quarter circles, and bisecting and trisecting the sixth parts in Ex. 63, giving twelfths, eighteenths, etc., of the whole circle. Also make these divisions on circles of various sizes, and on arcs in various positions. The eye will thus be trained to estimate readily any given part of a circumference.

CHAPTER V.

PROPORTIONAL ANGLES.

Principles.

AFTER acquiring power to draw lines, truly straight, in any direction, and to draw a true right angle in any position, much additional power of the eye to estimate, and of the hand to represent, will result from practice in estimating the values of the *angles* of objects. But we have seen that the right angle, upon which varied practice has now been had, is the natural standard of comparison for other angles. Hence the new group of valuable exercises which follow, is designed to train the learner in estimating and representing accurately any fractional part of a right angle in any position.

Every circle is considered as being divided into three hundred and sixty equal parts, called degrees and marked thus, 360°. Hence a half circle embraces 180°; a quarter circle, 90°; a sixth of a circle, 60°, etc. But, as already seen in the last chapter, two diameters at right angles to each other divide a circle into quarters; hence, as a right angle includes a quarter circle, or *arc* of 90°, between its sides, it is also called an *angle* of 90°.

In like manner, any angle is said to be an angle of as many degrees as there are in the arc between its sides, the centre of the arc being at the point or *vertex* of the angle. In other words an angle is said to be measured by the arc included between its sides. Hence the easiest way to divide an angle into equal parts, or parts having any given proportion to each other, is, to divide the arc between its sides in the manner required, and then to draw straight lines from these points of division to the vertex of the angle. The right angle being, as before explained, the natural angular measure for other angles, a right angle will be taken as the one to be variously divided, in the following examples.

Elementary Examples.

Ex. 66. Bisect a right angle, in each of the positions given in Ex. 33. To do this, sketch carefully a quarter circle between the sides of the angle and mark the middle point of this arc. Then join this middle point with the vertex of the angle as seen in the figure. To divide the angle into any other number of parts, divide the included quarter circle into the same number of parts. To test the angle thus estimated and drawn, use a "Protractor," as follows:

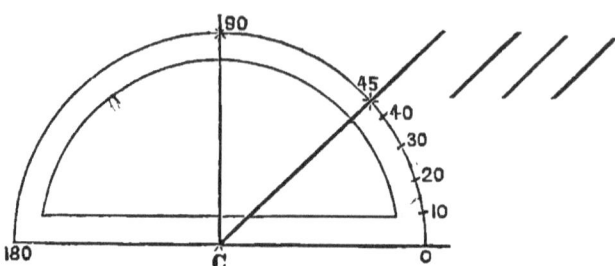

The protractor is a semi-circular instrument, whose semi-circular edge is divided into 180 degrees. A right angle is an angle of 90°. Half a right angle is 45°, hence if we place the straight side of the protractor on one side of the angle, and its centre, C, marked by a notch, at the point or *verter*, C, of the right angle, as shown in the figure, then the required bisecting line C, 45°, will if correct pass through the 45° point on the divided edge of the protractor. If it fails to do so, then first carefully estimate, *by the eye*, the amount of error, and then erase the line and draw it over, remembering to *sketch it lightly*, till found correct. Having found the true direction of the required dividing line of the given angle, *draw a number of parallels* to it, in this, and all the following problems of divisions of angles.

Ex. 67. Construct a line which will cut off *one-third* of a right angle from either of its sides, thus:

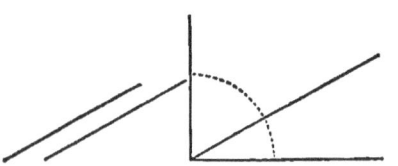 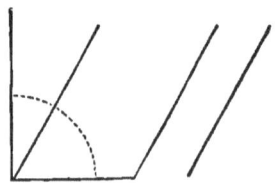

One-third of a right angle is 30°—measured by one-third of the quarter circle—hence in testing the lines after drawing them they should pass through the 30° point of the protractor in the first figure, and the 60° point in the second. In every case consider, as above, the number of degrees in the given fractional part of the right angle, and make the test accordingly.

In the figure, only two parallels to the required direction are shown. The student should make many more, and in various positions around the original figure.

Ex. 68. Draw a line cutting off *one-fourth* of a right angle from either of its sides. This can be most accurately done by bisecting half a right angle, thus:

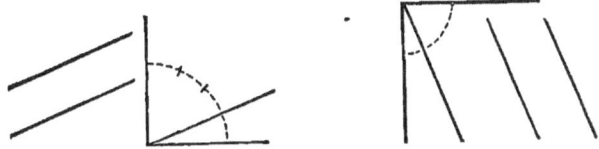

Observe, as indicated in these figures, to place the given right angle in any and all of the positions given in Ex. 33.

Ex. 69. Construct, successively, angles of *one-fifth*, and *two fifths* of a right angle; *i. e.*, angles of 18°, etc., thus:

Ex. 70. Divide a right angle into two parts, one of 40° the other of 50°. This can be most easily done by finding one-third of the right angle, and making the angle and arc of 40°, one-third greater than the one of 30°, thus:

Ex. 71. Repeat the divisions of the right angle, given in the

preceding examples, upon right angles in various oblique positions as in Ex. 36.

Practical Examples.

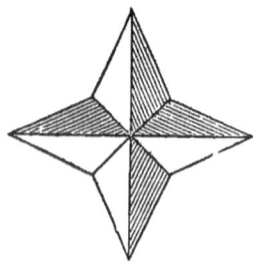

Ex. 72. A four pointed star, requiring two lines at right angles to each other, and the equal bisecting lines of those angles.

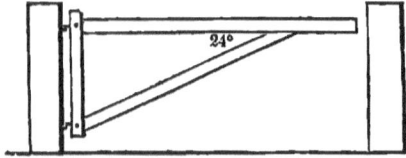

Ex. 73. A gate. Note that an angle of 24° is four-fifteenths of a right angle.

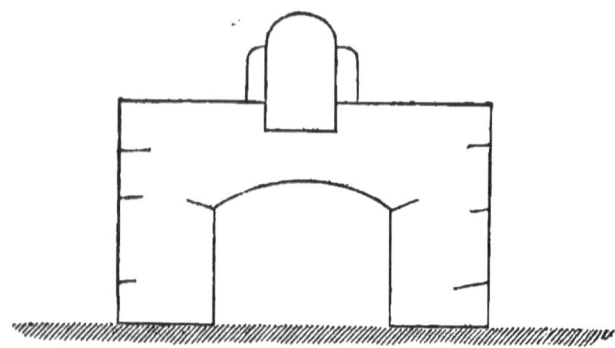

Ex. 74. An arch, giving practice in parallels, equal distances (each side of the arch, and the heights at the ends) and arcs, of various sizes, and parts of a circle.

CHAPTER VI.

PLANE FIGURES BOUNDED BY STRAIGHT LINES.

Principles.

A *plane figure* is a portion of a flat surface, bounded by lines When bounded by straight lines, it is called a *polygon*.

Polygons are of various names, depending on their number of sides.

A Triangle has the least possible number of sides, viz., three. It has also three angles, and when one of these is a right angle, the triangle is called *right angled*.

A Quadrilateral, or quadrangle, has four sides, and angles. When both the angles and sides are equal, the figure is a *square*, and its angles are all equal. When the angles are right angles, but only the opposite sides are equal, the figure is called a rectangle.

A *Pentagon* is a figure of five sides. In a *regular* pentagon the sides and angles are all equal.

Likewise, a regular *Hexagon* has six equal sides and angles.

The diagonal of a four-sided figure joins its opposite corners, thus: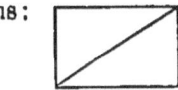

Figures of more than four sides, have more than one diagonal from any one corner.

The student is now prepared to sketch such simple objects as depend only on certain proportions between their angles.

According to the theory of beauty of angular proportions, briefly alluded to in Chapter II., those regular figures are most beautiful, in which the proportions of the angles can be expressed by fractions whose terms are small numbers.

A great many familiar objects have sides of an oblong, that is a *rectangular* form, and these sides are divided by their diagonals into two equal right angled triangles. A triangle is the simplest plane figure, and *a right angled triangle is the simplest triangle, as a standard for the comparison of angular proportions*, since it contains a right angle, which is the natural measure with which to compare its other angles.

Rectangles, as floors, walls, doors, windows, the spaces between them, etc., are therefore, most beautifully proportioned, *when their diagonals divide their right angles into parts bearing* a simple proportion to each other and to a right angle.

Thus, if the diagonal of a rectangle divides one of its right angles into angles of 30° and 60°, the ratio of these is $\frac{1}{2}$, and their ratios to a right angle, are $\frac{1}{3}$ and $\frac{2}{3}$. These all being simple fractions, the rectangle will be found to have agreeable proportions.

Elementary Examples.

The construction of regular figures, requires attention to the equality of some or all of the sides, as in Chapter III., as well as to their direction, and the proper size of their angles; and thus requires the application of examples in all the preceding chapters.

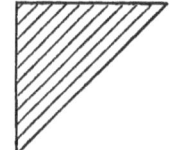 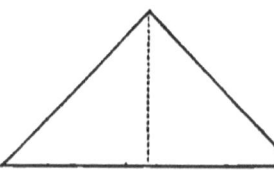

Ex. 75. A right angled triangle with equal acute angles of 45° each.

This triangle possesses the property of being divided by a perpendicular from its right angle to its opposite side, into two triangles of the same shape as the original whole. This property makes its construction easy. Draw this triangle in various positions, and fill it with lines parallel to its longest side, as above.

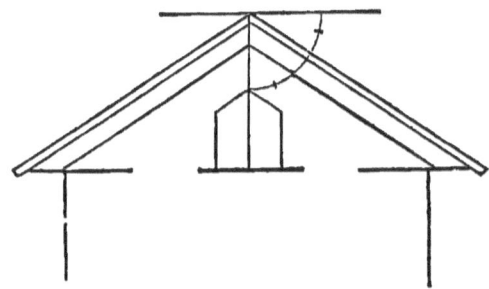

Ex. 76. A triangle each of whose halves is a right angled

PLANE FIGURES BOUNDED BY STRAIGHT LINES.   29

triangle with acute angles of 36° and 54°. Here $\frac{36°}{54°}=\frac{2}{3}$; $\frac{36°}{90°}=\frac{2}{5}$ and $\frac{54°}{90°}=\frac{3}{5}$. Also in the whole triangle $\frac{36°}{108°}=\frac{1}{3}$. These ratios being varied, while all of them are simple, the triangle is very pleasing and forms an agreeable end, or "pediment," to a roof, as seen in the figure.

Ex. 77. An equal sided triangle. This also, has equal angles of 60° each, and its halves therefore have acute angles of 30° and 60°. Draw several such triangles, and fill each one of some of them with one or more sets of lines, parallel, or perpendicular, to some one of its sides.

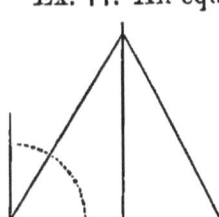

Ex. 78. Construct squares of various sizes and in various positions, first without their diagonals and then with them.

Ex. 79. A figure of four equal sides, but whose opposite angles, only, are equal, is called a Rhombus, thus:

This figure is most easily constructed by first drawing its diagonals so that each shall be at right angles to the other at its middle point, and by then joining their extremities.

Let rhombuses of various proportions be drawn.

A square may also be drawn by its diagonals in the same way.

Ex. 80. After the practice thus far had, various designs in plane figures can be executed, such as the following. These

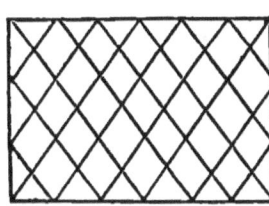 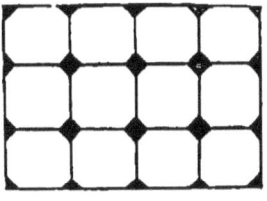

examples obviously require the divisions of lines into equal parts. Also, in the second figure, the marking of equal distances, viz., the semi-diagonals of the little squares.

Ex. 81. Embraces a regular pentagon and some applications of it.

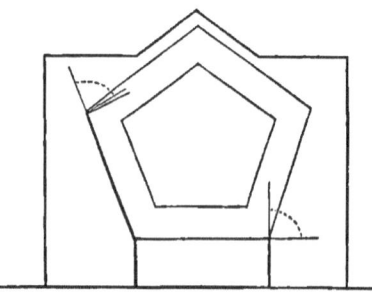 

The external angles of a pentagon formed by producing or extending its sides, are each equal to 72°, or four-fifths of a right angle, and are constructed accordingly. The five pointed star is most agreeably proportioned, by joining the alternate points in order to obtain the direction of the sides of the star points. Also, the middle line of any point, when extended, becomes the dividing line between the two opposite points.

Ex. 82. Hexagons. These polygons have angles of 120° at their corners. They can therefore be combined as in pavements, so as to completely fill a given space. It will assist in constructing this figure, to remember that each of its sides is equal to the distance from its corners to its centre. Observe, also, that the

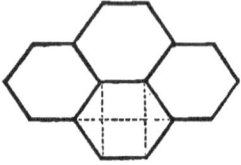

longer diagonal is divided into four equal parts by the shorter ones, perpendicular to it, and the centre.

Ex. 83. Divide a circle into eight equal parts, by diameters at 45° with each other, and join the points of division by straight lines, which will give a regular *octagon*, or eight sided figure. This figure can also be drawn, by considering that its external angles are each equal to 45°, thus:

PLANE FIGURES BOUNDED BY STRAIGHT LINES. 31

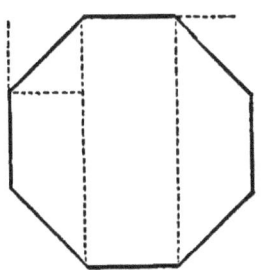

Practical Examples.

Ex. 84. Wholly made up of vertical and horizontal lines.

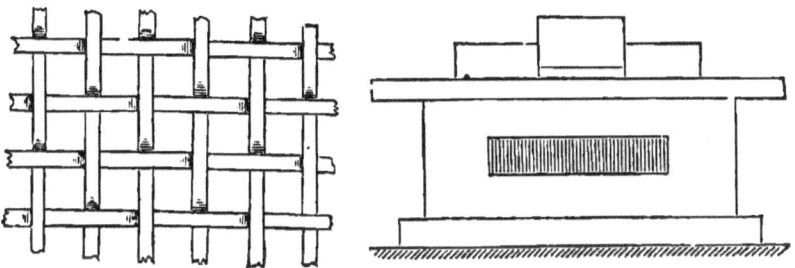

Ex. 85. Embraces oblique lines.

Ex. 86. Embraces circular lines.

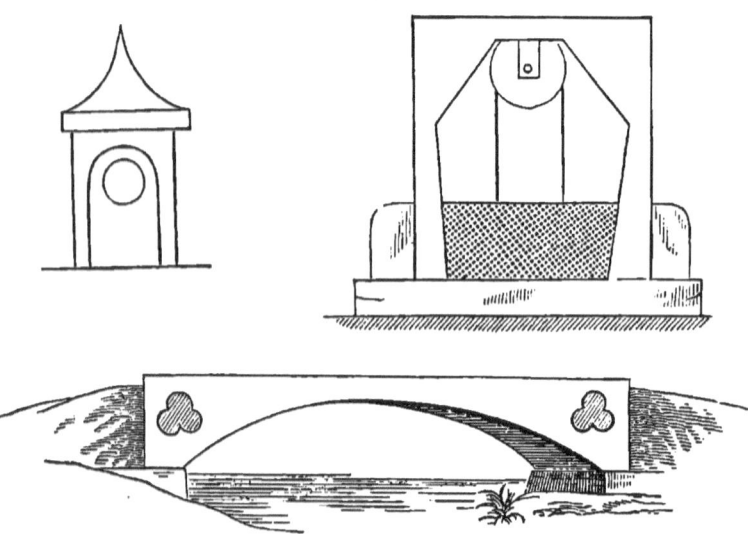

The figures of interlacing lines are best made by sketching the whole in *very faint*, and *unbroken* lines, at first; after which those portions of each line, which are meant to be visible, can be retraced in firm and heavy strokes.

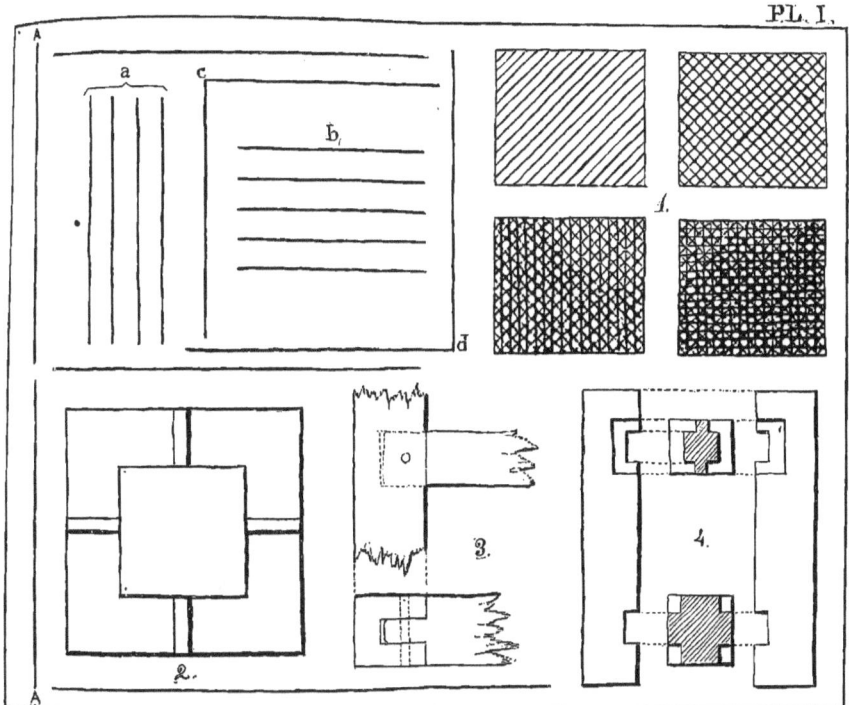

PL. I.

PL. II

CHAPTER VII.

RECTILINEAR AND CIRCULAR COMBINATIONS.

Principles.

WE gain, from observation of ornamental figures, and notably from that entertaining instrument, the kaleidoscope, certain *ideas*, which we will call those of *unity, symmetry*, and *variety*, in connection with figures compounded of a greater or less number of simple elements.

These ideas, all of which are pleasing, we will now proceed to explain, and illustrate.

UNITY is that property of a figure by which, although composed of parts, its parts are so linked together that it addresses the mind as *one* figure, and not as a collection of separate things. Thus three detached lines are naturally regarded as three separate things; but, as combined in a triangle, perfectly enclosing a space, they are naturally thought of as forming one thing, the triangle. So also, with the figures in the kaleidoscope, their regular arrangement around a single central point, gives them unity, so that we think of each as *one* figure.

SYMMETRY is *single, double*, or *multiple*.

A figure has *single* symmetry when it is divisible by only one line into two parts which will coincide when folded together about that line. Thus a butterfly has such symmetry, his wings coinciding, when folded together about the centre line of his back. Also any triangle, two of whose sides are equal, has a single line of symmetry, as AC in the next figure.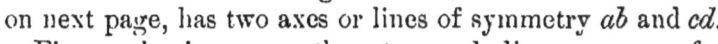

A figure has *double* symmetry, when it is divisible by two lines in the manner just described. Thus the rectangle ABCD, shown on next page, has two axes or lines of symmetry *ab* and *cd*.

Figures having more than two such lines, or axes, of symmetry, have multiple symmetry. Thus a square has four, two of which are its diagonals, and a circle has an infinite number, all its diameters being its lines of symmetry.

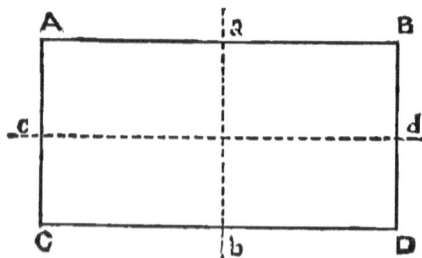

By VARIETY we here mean precisely what takes place in turning the kaleidoscope, that is, the pleasing result of different combinations of the same given elements.

The figures on plates III., IV., and V., will illustrate the ideas of *unity*, *symmetry* and *variety*, as here explained, and will afford examples of combination, suggesting many others.

Illustration. We have, first, eight different combinations of four equal right-angled triangles.

The first, Pl. III. Fig. 1, has *unity* in the close union of the triangles, but lacks symmetry, and is thus less pleasing than Fig. 7 which possesses both, though having only single symmetry.

Fig. 3 is without *symmetry* and is weak in *unity*, its parts being only united at a point, and is of inferior beauty.

Fig. 2 has *double symmetry*, but is weak in *unity*, the triangles being joined by their shorter sides. It is thus less pleasing than Fig. 4, where unity is more strongly expressed, by the union of the longer sides.

Figs. 5 and 6 both have *double symmetry*; Fig. 5 satisfies the idea of *unity* by means of its unbroken circumference, and Fig. 6 does the same by its solid union of the triangles. Both are pleasing, as is more apparent in case of Fig. 6, by drawing it as in Fig. 8, where the double lines, marking intermediate bands between the triangles, add richness to the figure.

Exercises.

From the above full illustration, the learner can proceed to invent as many combinations as possible, of the following sets of figures.

Ex. 87. Make various combinations of four equal acute isosceles triangles. See one in Pl. III., Fig. 9.

Ex. 88. Do the same with four equal obtuse isosceles triangles. See one in Pl. III., Fig. 10.

Ex. 89. Do. with four scalene triangles. See one in Pl. III., Fig. 11.

Ex. 90. Do. with four equal squares. See Pl. III., Fig. 12, for one.

Ex. 91. Do. with four equal rhombuses. See Pl. V., Fig. 1.

Ex. 92. Do. with four trapezoids; a figure of single symmetry with two parallel sides. See Pl. V., Fig. 2.

General Example. Vary the last six examples in one or more of the following ways:

(1) By increasing the number of figures to be combined, still keeping them equal.

(2) By making them unequal, but still similar, as in combining large and small rhombuses or trapezoids, as in Pl. V., Fig. 3, of rhombuses, where the eight angles around the central point are equal.

(3) By making the elementary figures unequal and dissimilar, or at least dissimilar, as in Pl. V., Fig. 5, a pendant composed of right angled, acute angled, and obtuse angled triangles; Fig. 4 a decorative cross, and Fig. 6, of various rhombuses-like figures of single symmetry (or mono-symmetrical, they may be called).

Fig. 5 may be supplemented by additions, like the one shown, at each of the three remaining corners of the square; and may be varied by other arrangements of the pendant triangle, or by using other figures.

PLATE IV. shows other examples of symmetry and varied combination based upon a square foundation.

Ex. 93. Fig. 1 shows a doubly symmetrical arrangement of four-sided figures of single symmetry.

Ex. 94. Fig. 2 shows the variation of Fig. 1, by placing the right angles of its component figures at the centre. Both arrangements might alternate in the same figure; which would then better be placed diagonally.

Ex. 95. In Fig. 3, a combination of squares, the sides of each making angles of 45° with the next, the angles of each might have extended beyond the circumference of the next outer one.

Ex. 96. Fig. 4 might be varied by many different ways of occupying the angles between the equal arms of the cross.

Exs. 97–98. Figs 5, 6, each give but one-half of a figure of single symmetry, the whole figure to be drawn by the student.

Exs. 99–101. Figs. 7, 8, 9, are mostly composed of circular elements, arranged upon a foundation circle, the *first*, a rosette of six points ; the *second*, having the centres of the looped arcs at the angles of the curved quadrangle ; the *last*, the centres of the outer arcs of any leaf, at the extremities of the diameter which passes through the next leaf.

By means of the suggestions attached to these examples, the learner will readily find the path of discovery leading to new designs, as well as to other variations of those here given.

The figures of Pl. IV., may well be drawn of such size that four, or even two of them will fill the plate.

The use of the segments of centre lines, as in Figs. 2, 8, 9, serves to give vividness to the figures by emphasizing the qualities of unity and symmetry possessed by them. This will become more evident by omitting them, and then comparing the results, for the same figure. See also, Fig. 3, where the blank centre weakens the expression of unity.

Ex. 102. Combine circles by interlacing, as in Pl. V., Fig. 7. Also with their centres arranged on a circle.

CHAPTER VIII.

Curves and Curved Objects in General.

WE have thus far mostly considered circular curves. These, however, are only the simplest among an endless diversity of curves, many of which are of great beauty, as well as common usefulness.

When any curve and straight line merely touch at one point, they are said to be tangent to each other, and just at the point of touch, or *tangency, they lie in the same direction.* Hence *any curve can be much more easily sketched, if we know several tangents to it at different points.*

A circle can evidently be placed, or "*inscribed*" in a square, so as to be tangent to it at the middle point of each side. A curve similarly inscribed in a rectangle is called an *ellipse*. Now observe that as all squares are of the same shape, though of different sizes, so all circles must be of the same shape, also. But there is an endless variety in the proportions of different rectangles, and hence there may be an equal variety of ellipses.

A right angle being more easily estimated than other angles, *it is also a special help, in sketching a curve, to have one or more lines which the curve must cross at right angles.* Hence it will be easier to sketch an ellipse in a rhombus than in a rectangle; for in the former, the ellipse will be tangent to the four sides, and will cross each diagonal, at right angles with it, and at equal distances from its extremities.

Ex. 103. Sketch ellipses of various proportions by the rhomboidal method, thus: Mark the middle point of each side, as

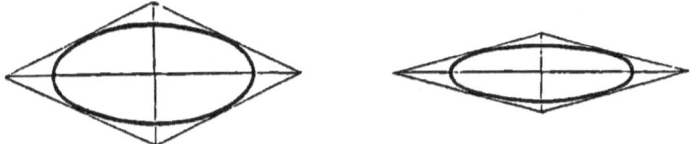

points of tangency of the ellipse; then, make each diagonal of the rhombus, the diagonal of a square containing an inscribed circle, which will cross those diagonals at other points of the ellipse.

Let this exercise be continued, in the sketching of ellipses in rhombuses placed in various oblique positions, and, also, with their longer diagonals placed vertically.

When an ellipse is inscribed in a rectangle, it crosses the centre lines of the rectangle at right angles, at the points of tangency with the sides of the rectangle. Thus the eight guiding positions afforded by the rhombus, are reduced by union to four, in the rectangle. The ellipse will, however, cross the diagonals of a rectangle at equal distances from its corners, but not in a perpendicular direction.

Ex. 104. Sketch ellipses in rectangles and other figures, of various proportions and positions, thus:

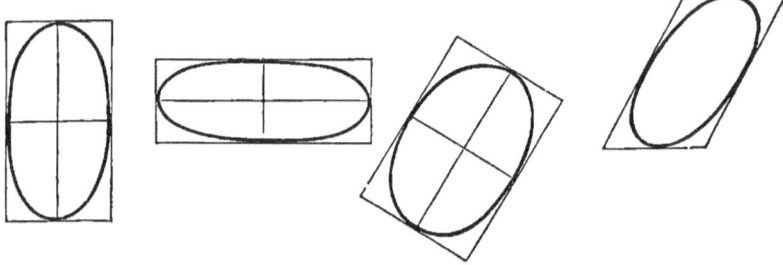

An ellipse is a curve of most delicate grace, and should therefore be most faithfully studied and carefully drawn. The most offensive error in shaping it, is, to represent it as pointed at the narrow end, which it is not, in the least.

By combining elliptical arcs of various proportions, tangent to each other, various graceful forms adapted to ornaments, such as vases, may be composed. In doing this the relative proportions of the ellipses should not be chosen at random, but so that the angles of their enclosing rhombuses should form simple ratios. Moreover, these rhombuses should be in simple relative positions, and the corresponding angles in the different ones should form simple ratios.

Ex. 105. In this design for a vase, all the angles, some of whose degrees are given in the enclosed numbers, are 9°, the *square* of 9°, or *even multiples* of 9°. Also at the base, two rhombuses have a common vertex; and at top, two have a side and two

CURVES AND CURVED OBJECTS IN GENERAL. 39

vertices in common. The acute rim-rhombus has its sides perpendicular to a 54 and b 72, its right side passes through the corner 72, and its diagonal passes through c, the junction of two arcs, and centre of a 72. Moreover, the diagonal 72–36 coincides with 18–72 produced, and the side 72–54 is parallel to the diagonal 18–36.

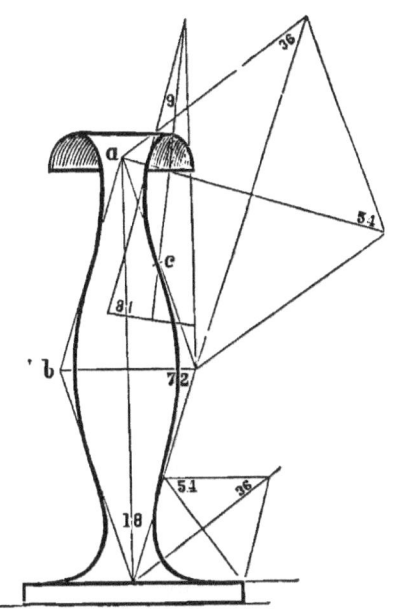

These mostly very simple relations of the rhombuses, and their angles, yield a very pleasing form, each side of which embraces four different elliptical arcs, of which the one running upward from c terminates on a 54.

Ex. 106. In this design, the relations are in part, more, and in part less simple than in the preceding, and the result will hardly be thought more agreeable than before.

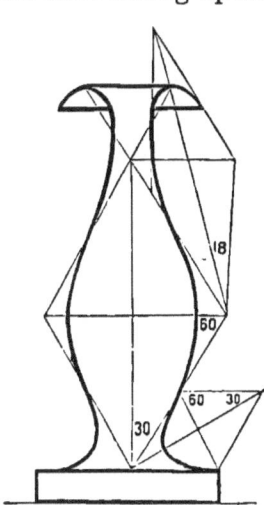

The principal, and the base rhombuses are of the same proportions, as seen by their angles, and therefore enclose similar ellipses, which gives less decided variety in the outline at the base. The upper side-rhombus, with its angle of 18°, side of one in the central rhombus of 60°, gives the comparatively complex and unfamiliar ratio $\frac{3}{10}$. Also its right hand corner is arbitrarily located on a horizontal line through the upper vertex of the central rhombus.

In both of these designs the rolling rim might be omitted by terminating the sides of the vases on the longer diagonals of the narrow upper side rectangles.

Ex. 107. By substituting for a rhombus, two dissimilar half

rhombuses, having a diagonal in common, the beautiful egg shaped curve will be formed, thus:

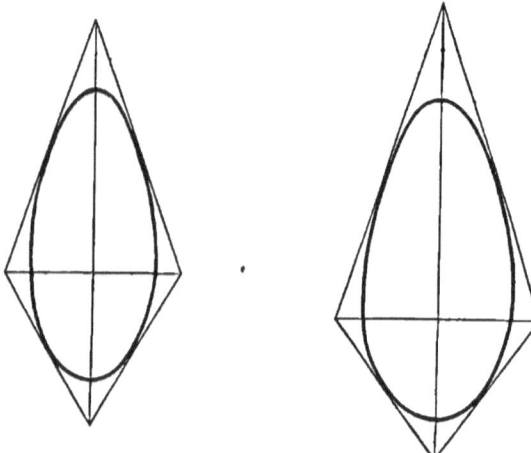

In the first of these figures, the acute half angles are 20° and 30°, whose ratio is therefore ⅔. In the second figure the corresponding angles are 18° and 36°, having therefore a ratio of ½, and affording a more decidedly egg-shaped curve.

Ex. 108. An egg-shaped oval may also be inscribed in a regular trapezoid, that is a figure having two unequal but parallel sides, both of which are bisected by the same line, perpendicular to both, thus:

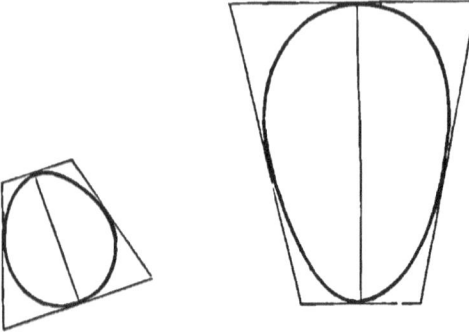

Let these ovals be drawn in a great variety of proportions and positions, both in rhombus-like figures and trapezoids, *and with as frequent reference as possible to leaves*, which exhibit a great variety of graceful ovals.

Ex. 109. The material of vases, etc., being originally plastic, it may be supposed to settle by its own weight into oval forms before hardening. For this reason, as well as from the greater stability associated with breadth at base, egg forms are more admired in pottery articles than true ellipses. The annexed design illustrates these remarks. Its angles of 36° and 54°; 54° and 10°-48′ (ten degrees and forty-eight minutes) 75°-36′ and 18°-54′, give the simple ratios $\frac{2}{8}$, $\frac{1}{5}$, $\frac{1}{7}$, $\frac{1}{4}$. The student should make a variety of similar designs.

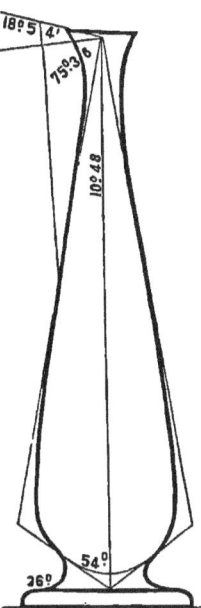

Examples 105, 106, 109, are here incidental and preliminary, illustrating a manner of using ellipses and ovals by means of circumscribed rhombuses, etc. The use of ovals in designs will be more fully and systematically explained in Part III.

Ex. 110. On account of the pleasing associations of stability and decision with horizontal and vertical lines, as indicated in Chap. I., a curve which enters into the composition of any solid and fixed object is most pleasing when it has one or more horizontal or vertical tangents.

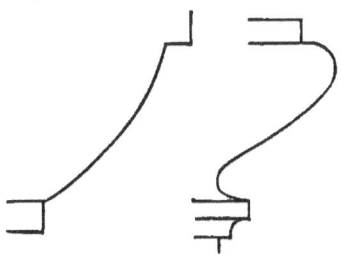

Thus, there is more vigor, as well as variety, in the curve in the second of these figures, than in the first.

Ex. 111. As we here propose only such exercises as are more closely associated with geometrical drawing, we only allude to

the careful drawing of German text and common writing (script) letters on a large scale, as an excellent exercise in the close study and varied practice of drawing curves.

The German text, and all upright letters should be evenly balanced on each side of an imaginary vertical centre line, in order to give them the most satisfactory appearance.

Ex. 112. The varieties of curves being innumerable, a few are here annexed by way of suggestion. The student can devise many others.

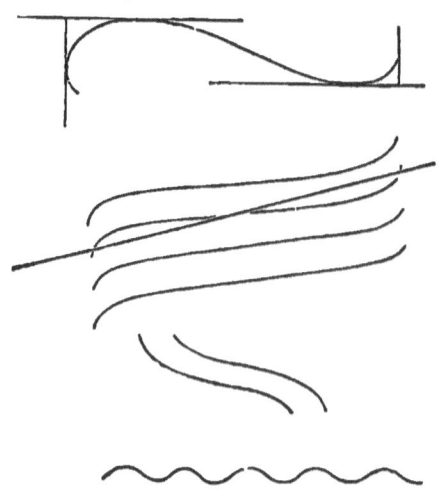

The group of four parallel curves affords an excellent example for practice, each curve being nearly straight in the middle, and sharply curved at the ends, while its left-hand half is convex upwards, and its right-hand half equally so downwards; and each with a vertical tangent at its extremities.

Of the two spirals, it will be seen that one increases its radius uniformly, giving equal radial distances between its successive turns, while the other expands at an increasing rate.

The use of tangents in sketching curves is also illustrated in these examples.

Ex. 113. *An exercise of peculiar utility*, is found in sketching easy curves through several given scattered points. This operation frequently occurs in geometrical drawing, when other than

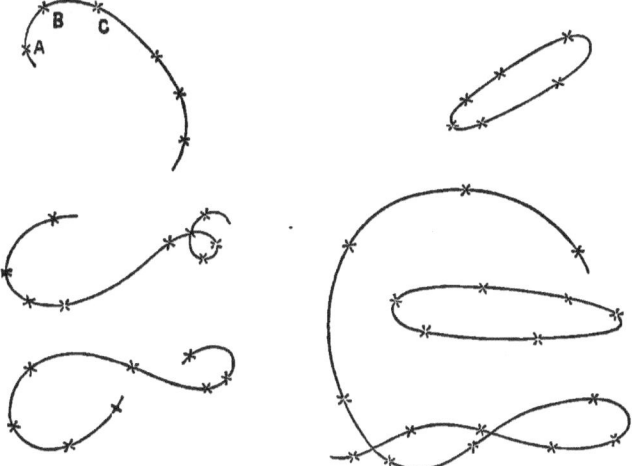

circular curves are to be described. The essential things to be observed in these cases, are, *first*, to avoid all sudden, irregular, and unnecessary variations in the rate or degree of curvature, and, *second*, especially to avoid making an angle at any point in the intended curve. These important requirements can be met by keeping at least *three* successive points in view at once. Thus, while joining A and B in the figure, keep C in view, and operate likewise in making all similar figures.

The student should practice extensively on this example, *first taking the points*, in many different relative positions, and then running easily flowing curves through them.

Ex. 114. In several of the preceding examples, curves have been drawn tangent to straight lines previously drawn. We here add an example of drawing tangents to curves already drawn.

The tangent may be drawn through a given point out of the curve, as in the first figure, or through a given point on the curve as in the second figure.

Ex. 115. Finally, the examples of this chapter close with practice in the very nice operation of drawing symmetrical figures with variously curved outlines. Symmetrical figures (p. 33), are those which are divided in one or more ways, by a centre line, into similar halves, as in this figure. The difficulty in such figures, after forming one side in a pleasing curve, is, to make the other side of exactly the same form, but in a reversed position. This can be done, as in the figure, by drawing lines perpendicular to the centre line, and by marking on them equal distances on each side of the centre line. The following are other examples of symmetrical figures, some of which have two centre lines. The learner can devise many other figures of similar character.

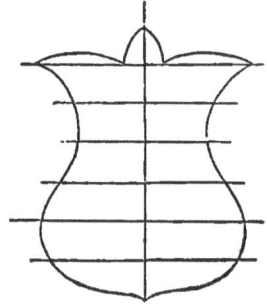

Ex. 116. Let Pl. IV., Figs. 10, 11, each be taken as one half of a symmetrical figure, and draw the other half.

CURVES AND CURVED OBJECTS IN GENERAL. 45

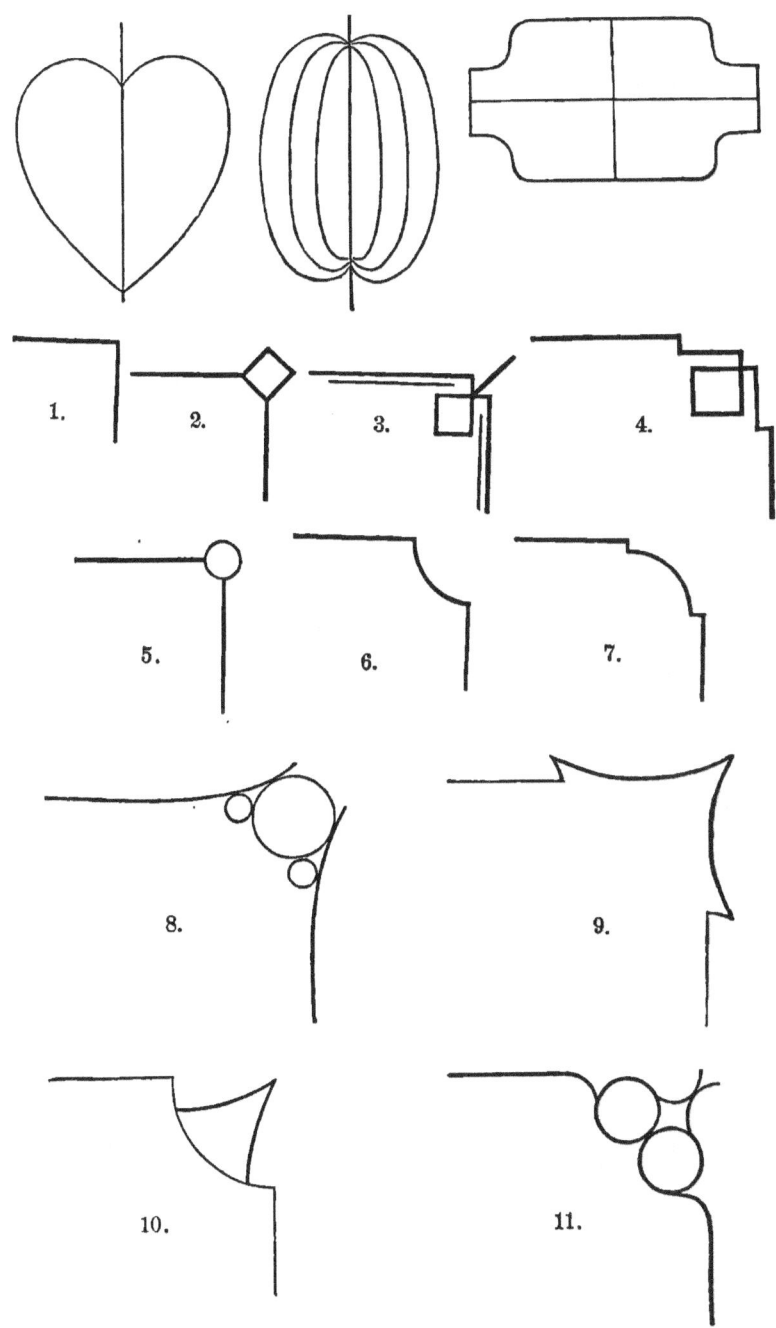

Ex. 117. Representing a few elementary corner pieces, illustrates some of the foregoing principles. 10 is inferior to 9 because its main spur seems weakly placed, or driven in, while the spurred corner, 9, is firmly planted. 7 is better than 6, because it cuts out less of the interior, and because the grace of the curve is protected by the strength of the square corners at each side of it.

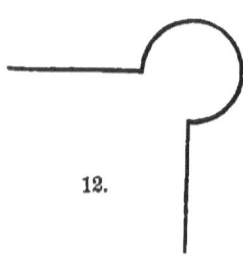

12.

Thus the *skeleton* of every corner should embody a *good idea*, for no richness of detail in ornament can redeem bad governing outlines.

Attention to such simple principles as these will guide in the design or selection of borders, and prevent the necessity of presenting an elaborate collection of them here, when they can be seen in such abundance in type-founders' collections, and in engravers' and printers' works, together with various ornamental devices.

Another principle, disregard of which through disproportionate interest in some trivial thing, may spoil a good drawing, is this. Ornamental devices on drawings of solid worth, should never represent anything essentially mean, or rudely comic, or even anything of merely transient interest. Neither should they be attempted unless they are sure to be well executed.

Thus, a vignette on a map of a survey may contain a sketch of some pretty view seen from some point. A drawing of an engineering structure or a machine, may contain a pictorial view of the same object; or of the establishment where it was made, or of the room or building in which the drawing was made; anything in short, which is agreeable in itself, and not foreign to the subject.

Ex. 118. As a concluding exercise upon useful symmetrical figures, various ornamental arrow, or spear heads may be drawn. See Pl. V., Fig. 8. These are useful in iron-work, and as devices for vanes, and as indicating the meridian in maps of surveys.

PL. III.

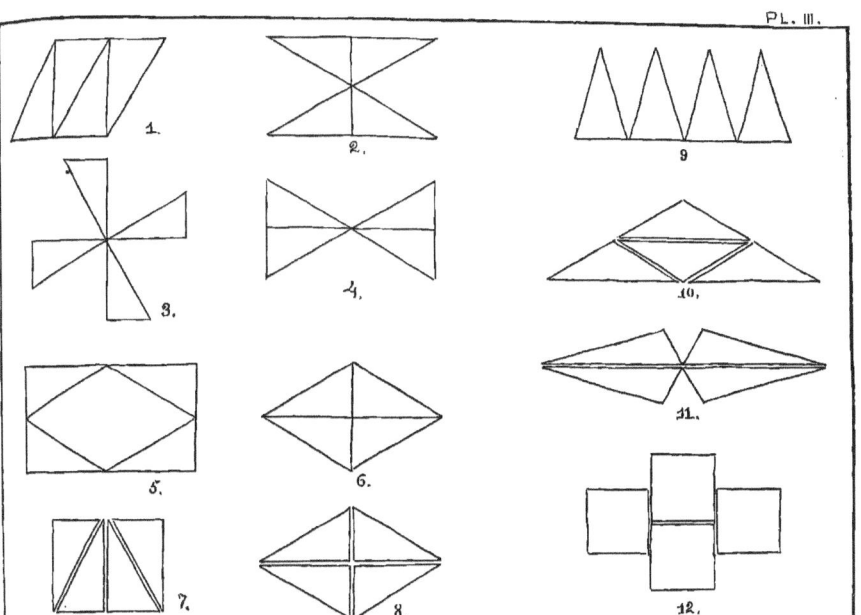

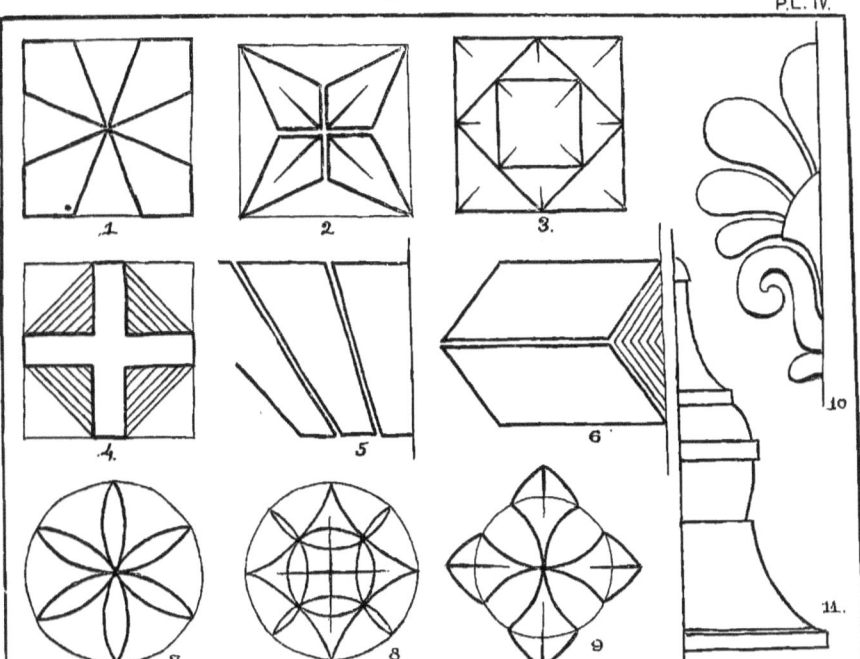

P.L. IV.

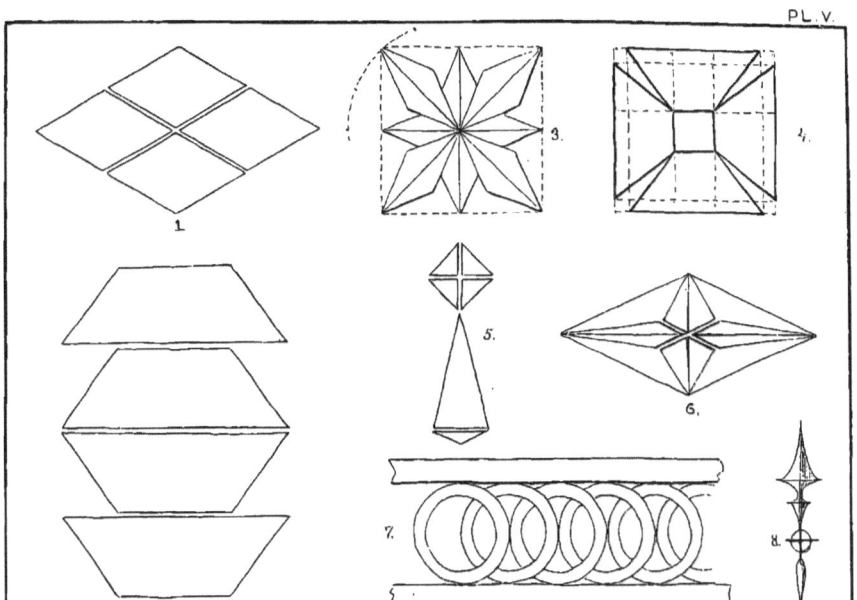

CHAPTER IX.

LETTERING.

General Principles.

LETTERING, though not strictly a part of a drawing, is a necessary appendage to it, it being generally indispensable to the full understanding and intended use of the drawing. And as, also, there should be uniformity of accuracy and elegance in all parts of the draftsman's work, lettering is properly included among the fundamental operations, which he should be familiar with before applying his art in practical cases.

Besides, although geometrical drawings should be principally titled with geometrical letters, yet these letters are, on account of their usually moderate size, as well as variety and curvature of outline, most conveniently made by the free hand. Hence the draftsman's training in lettering appropriately falls among the subjects of free geometrical drawing.

Two points should be constantly remembered during the practice of lettering: *first, uniformity* of size and proportions, and, *second*, beauty and regularity of form in each letter. Ill-shaped letters, if of uniform size, proportions, and distance apart, and truly ranged in a straight line or regular curve, will look tolerably neat. Elegant letters will, on the other hand, appear badly, if irregularly sized and located. Both uniformity, and elegance are, therefore, indispensable to perfect lettering.

The learner's previous practice, in marking equal and proportional distances and angles, should enable him to secure uniformity in his letters; and his practice on curved and other irregular lines and figures, should enable him to give them elegance of form.

All the letters described in this chapter should first be drawn on plates of smooth heavy brown paper, about 11 by 14 inches in size, and with a crayon or soft pencil. They should be made three or four inches high, so as to afford exercise in free and broad movements of the hand, and may afterwards be made of ordinary sizes, on smaller plates, and in title pages.

Roman Capitals.

Before entering upon a general discussion of all the varieties of letters, we will make a special study of the common Roman capital letter, which is a sort of standard which all other letters are made to resemble, more or less closely, in certain particulars; and from which, as a starting point, variations are made in designing fanciful letters.

PLATE VI. *The Alphabet in Large Roman Capitals.*—This alphabet is arranged in three groups, so as to form progressive exercises in the drawing of the letters. The first group embraces those letters such as I and H, etc., which are composed, wholly or mostly, of *horizontal* and *vertical straight lines*. The second group contains all those letters in which *oblique straight lines* are prominent; while the third group embraces those letters which are largely made up of *curved lines*.

Letters, as large as those of this plate, may be made by instruments, by observing certain proportions in their form; but, inasmuch as, in common practice, letters are of such size that they are more conveniently made by hand, it will be far better for the student to make the large letters of Pl. VI. by hand, at least so far as to sketch their curved lines, and the points through which their straight lines pass; after which, the lines, if inked, may be ruled. A running commentary on the different letters of Pl. VI. will now be sufficient. I, the simplest of all the letters, consists of a vertical column, whose width may properly be made equal to a quarter of its entire height. The caps at the top and bottom project beyond the column a distance on each side, equal to half the width of the column. These proportions may be observed in the wide parts and caps of all the letters.

We thus have for an I the following complete proportions: Divide its height into sixteen equal parts. Then its height = $\frac{16}{16}$, its total width $\frac{8}{16}$, width of column $\frac{4}{16}$, projection of cap $\frac{2}{16}$, and thickness of cap $\frac{1}{16}$. These dimensions are to be preserved in the vertical columns of all the letters. Also all wide columns are to be of $\frac{4}{16}$ *perpendicular* width, and all the caps are to be $\frac{1}{16}$ thick.

Having thus fixed upon a proper thickness for the caps, let lines be ruled parallel to the extreme top and bottom lines, to aid in making these caps of uniform thickness on all the letters

Each column of the H is like an I. The extreme width of this letter allowing $\frac{1}{16}$ between the caps is equal to $\frac{17}{16}$ of its total height.

The height of the arm of the L is $\frac{7}{16}$ of the total height of the letter. The extreme width of this letter, and of F, making the arms $\frac{1}{16}$ longer than they are high, is $\frac{14}{16}$ of the height. The ends of the arms must be $\frac{1}{16}$ thick. F is like an L turned upside down, with the addition of the middle arm, whose height is half the height of the letter, and whose right-hand line is midway between the right-hand line of the column and the extreme right-hand line of the letter. E differs from F only in having another arm. Some designers make this letter a little wider ($\frac{14}{16}$) at bottom than at the top, and also make the height of the top arm a little less than that of the lower one. This method gives variety and an appearance of stability.

T, having an arm on each side of a central column, has its extreme width equal $\frac{18}{16}$ of its total height. Notice, on all these arms, that their curved sides are nearly quarter circles, giving solidity of appearance to the arms. None of these arms should be short, thin, or pointed.

Passing the hyphen we come to letters having oblique elements. V having its *average* width only equal to half its extreme width, since it comes nearly to a point at one extremity, may be made of extra width at the top; thus, let the total width be such as would be given by two wide columns with $\frac{14}{16}$ between their caps. This width will then be $\frac{18\frac{1}{2}}{16}$ of the whole height. Let the perpendicular width of all narrow columns be $\frac{1}{16}$, and the horizontal width of V and A at their points $\frac{1\frac{1}{2}}{16}$.

Observe, that the left hand column is the wide one, and that in all letters having slanting columns, except Z, the heavy column slants *downward* towards the *right*. Similar general directions to the preceding, apply to A. The cross bar of this letter may be half way from the bottom line to the inner angle. In K the under side of the narrow arm may intersect the vertical column, a little below the middle, as at two-fifths of its height, so that the wide oblique column may not intersect the vertical column. The extreme width at the top equals the total height, and at the bottom equals $\frac{17\frac{1}{2}}{16}$ of the whole height.

N, having an oblique wide column, but being a square letter, having two vertical columns, does not need the extra width given to V and A. The length of full caps to oblique wide columns being $\frac{8\frac{1}{2}}{16}$, and to vertical narrow ones $\frac{5}{16}$, the total width at top, allowing $\frac{1}{16}$ between caps, if there were a full cap at the left upper corner, will be $\frac{14\frac{1}{2}}{16}$. There is no cap at the lower right-hand corner.

The under edge of its wide column is drawn from the left side of the foot of the right-hand narrow column, tangent to the slight curve which connects the upper left-hand cap with the left-hand narrow column. M has its total width equal to $\frac{21}{16}$ of its total height. The point of the V-shaped part is on the bottom line, and midway between the inner lines of the adjacent vertical columns. W, the widest letter of the alphabet, is of an extreme width equal to $\frac{27\frac{1}{2}}{16}$ of its extreme height. Its oblique lines are parallel to the corresponding lines of V. The extreme width of Z is equal to $\frac{14\frac{1}{2}}{16}$ of the height. Its arms are lengthened, as there are no caps opposite to them. The lower one is $\frac{10}{16}$ long and $\frac{8}{16}$ high, the upper $\frac{9}{16}$ long and $\frac{7}{16}$ high.

The left-hand vertical lines of the left-hand caps of X are in a vertical line. Reckoning from these lines, the extreme width at bottom is equal to $\frac{15\frac{1}{2}}{16}$ of the total height, and at top it is equal to $\frac{14}{16}$ of the height. In Y the outer oblique lines intersect the vertical column a little below the middle, as at a distance equal to the thickness of the caps. The whole width at the top equals $\frac{17}{16}$ of the whole height.

Passing the second hyphen, we come now to letters in which curves form a prominent part. The total width of J is $\frac{11}{16}$ of its height. Its larger curve, convex downward, has for a chord a horizontal line, at a height above the bottom equal to $\frac{5\frac{1}{2}}{16}$ of the height. The extreme width of U is $\frac{14}{16}$, of D $\frac{16}{16}$, of P $\frac{15}{16}$, and B $\frac{15}{16}$, of the height. The bow of the P should intersect the column a little below the middle, while the upper bow of the B may properly intersect the column a little above the middle, making the lower bow project $\frac{1}{16}$ beyond the upper one. R is $\frac{16}{16}$ wide at bottom. It differs from B so little, as not to need further description. By omitting the tail of the Q it becomes an O. The greatest width of the tail equals that of a wide column, and it extends three-fourths of the same width below the body of the letter. In either case the extreme width equals $\frac{14}{16}$ of the height. The extreme width of C equals $\frac{15}{16}$. The highest and lowest points of its outer curve are in the middle of the extreme width; and the corresponding points of the inner curve are half way between the inner point of the lower curved arm and the vertical tangent to the inner curve. In a letter as large as this, it is well to let the upper arm set back, a distance equal to the thickness of a cap, so as to prevent the overhanging look that it otherwise would have. The extreme width of G equals its total height. Its construction is evident from the figure, after the description of C, that has been given. The whole width of S equals that of Q, and its arms are nearly like those of C. Some designers make the lower half higher and wider than the upper half, but as S is, to a beginner, the most troublesome letter, it is here given in its simplest form. To sketch it readily, it is only necessary to keep in mind that the outer curve at the top becomes the inner one in the lower half, and so must be carried below the middle of the letter and curved sharply to form the inner line of the lower half. & is less subject to rule than the proper letters of the alphabet. The design on Pl. I. is offered as being more pleasing than that in which the wing over the period ends in a rectangular cap. The dotted lines show a modification of the design, ending in a large circle.

The proportions here given are not absolute, but only relative. Thus an ordinary letter, as an H, or an E, may be made twice as wide as it is high, or half as wide as it is high, but in that case all the other letters would have similar modifications of their present proportions. Such letters are called, respectively, *expanded* and *condensed* letters.

Directions, much more minute than the preceding, are sometimes given for lettering, but, after affording a few essential hints concerning the general proportions of letters, it is here preferred to leave the details of their design to the taste and judgment of the designer.

Letters in General.

In examining a type-founder's specimen book, one may imagine, from the exceeding variety of letters therein exhibited, that it must be impossible to reduce them to any system. But a closer examination will reveal a few comprehensive features, according to which all letters may be readily classified in groups.

By acquaintance with the distinguishing characters of these groups, and their modes of variation from one another, it will be easy to design uniform letters in any proposed form or style, which is much better than a mere copying of them, without ability to proceed independently of a copy.

All letters may be included in two grand divisions.

I.—*Geometrical letters* are all those which have a definite geometrical outline, which, when sufficiently large, could be made with drawing instruments; and—

II.—*Free-hand letters*, or those of so irregularly varied outline that they must be made by hand only, guided mainly by the fancy of the designer.

Since the letters called geometrical are the ones mainly used in geometrical drawing, they will chiefly be noticed in this section. The student, by collecting a number of hand-bills, programmes, business cards, sheet-music covers, etc., will have materials for a valuable scrap-book of letters, which will be useful for reference, and will contain numerous practical illustrations of the explanations which follow.

By examining such a collection, it will be seen that in all ordinary letters three things may be distinguished—

(*a*) the *essential elements*.
(*b*) the *complementary additions*.
(*c*) the *decorations*.

The *essential elements* of letters, are those which are necessary, and sufficient, to enable one to recognize the letters. The first half of the first and third lines, and the second and fourth examples on the second line of Pl. VII., are letters formed of essential elements only.

The *complementary additions* are the caps, and the hanging parts of the arms, etc. The letters of the first five, and the seventh, lines of Pl. VII. are, with the exception of those just mentioned, letters having these additions.

By the *decorations* are meant the ornamental shading and filling up of the letters. Thus letters may be represented as if made of wood, stone, or iron; and of pieces having square or polygonal sections. They may appear as if seen obliquely, or as draped, vine-clad, or casting shadows.

In spacing letters, it is a good rule to allow equal areas of blank paper between them.

LETTERING.

Summing up; the preceding, and other particulars concerning letters, are systematically presented in the following table:—

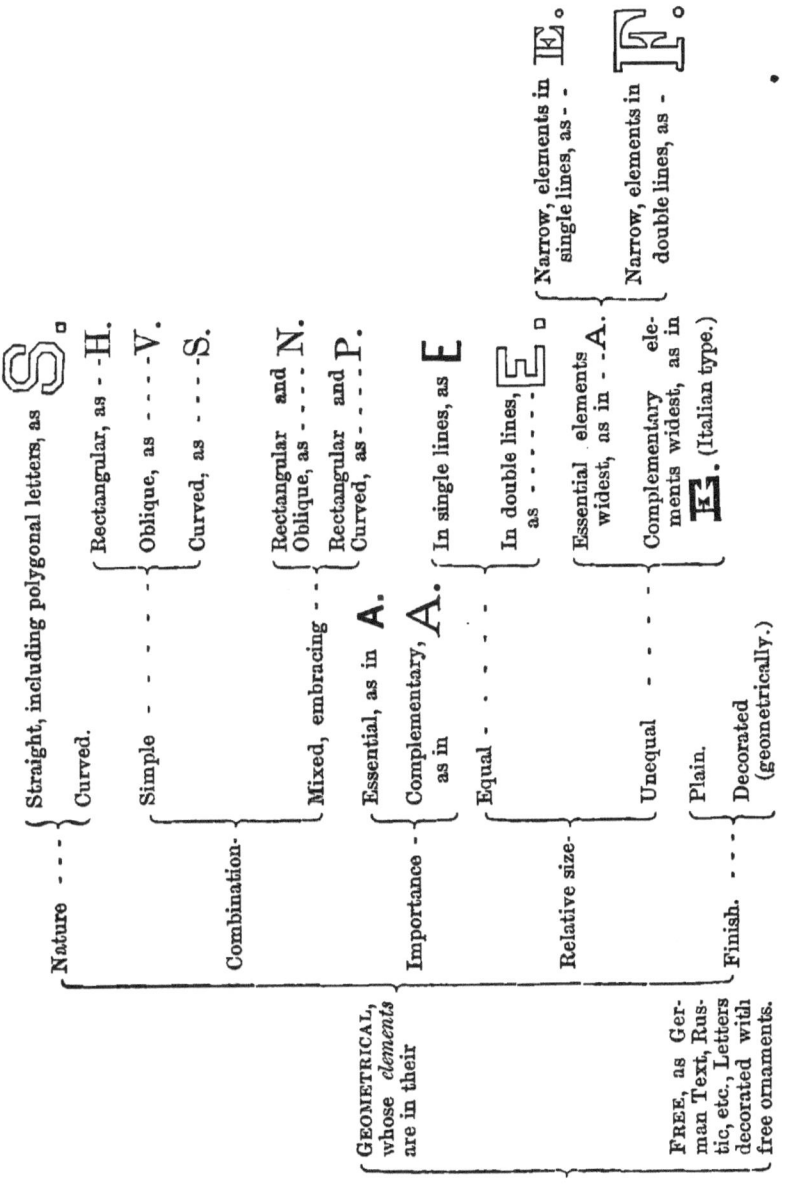

It follows from this, that there cannot be very many radically different forms of letters; therefore, instead of making a further subdivision of geometrical letters, some of the ways may be mentioned in which *varieties* of letters are produced by modifications of the elements just given.

1°. By altering the proportions of height and width, forming *expanded* or *condensed* letters.

2°. By retaining or omitting the complementary additions.

3°. By making the wide columns of the letter massive or slender.

4°. By making the letters as if they were flat plates, or as if they were solid, or "block" letters.

5°. By representing the latter as seen directly, or obliquely, so as to show both face and thickness.

6°. By minor modifications in the outlines, as by rounding the caps into the columns.

7°. By making the usually curved letters polygonal.

8°. Varieties, without limit, may be made, by changes in the quantity and character of the decorations.

Practical Remarks.

(*a.*) The thickness of the caps is the same as that of the narrow essential elements.

(*b.*) In pencilling letters, never pencil the ornaments, unless the letters are of extraordinary size, but pencil the outlines only, in very fine lines.

(*c.*) It is better to do all the pencilling by hand, since instruments would perpetually be hiding portions of the letters, and so preventing the eye from judging readily of their proper proportions.

(*d.*) Very small capitals and small letters are better put in off hand, in ink, between parallel pencil lines, to keep them of a uniform height.

(*e.*) The sixth row of Pl. IV. shows a simple free-hand or "rustic" letter, in two sizes and styles. These are *bark* letters. Log letters are often seen in handbills, etc.

(*f.*) The sixth row embraces "skeleton" and "full faced" "small" Roman letters and italics. A common error consists in making the stems of the b's, p's, etc., too long. The total height of such letters need not be more than one and a half times the height of their bodies.

(*g.*) To avoid making letters slightly leaning, stand directly in front of the work, and with the eyes far enough from the paper to be able to see the position of the border of the plate, as a guide. Or, rule vertical parallels at short intervals.

(*h.*) Curves can be more neatly sketched in by a dotting, or very light motion of the pencil, than by a continuous motion with firm pressure.

(*i.*) The ends of the arms of letters like G, C, S, etc., should not be far apart, vertically, but should come nearly together, and should be tangent to vertical lines, in order to give them a plump, finished, square, and stable look.

(*j.*) Even in the most fanciful letters, there is a certain appreciable consistency and orderly form. This results from their having an imaginary central skeleton of regular single lines, about which the outlines of their parts are equally balanced.

(*k.*) Pl. VII. illustrates most of the distinctions of form mentioned in the preceding table, except the inelegant and unused Italian type. This plate, or one of similar nature, should be constructed by the student.

(*l.*) Polygonal letters may be substituted for curved ones by any who are particularly deficient in free-hand sketching. They may thus be able to secure a desirable uniformity of excellence in their work; though it is probable that the pains necessary to form an elegant polygonal letter would secure an equally elegant curved one.

(*m.*) In line 2d, example 1*st* is elegant in being slightly expanded, and not heavy. Ex. 2*d* is neat and easy to make. In titles, the letters should be further apart. Ex. 3*d*, of this line and of line 7th, are partly Italian in character, the essential parts being lightest. Ex. 4*th*, is like Ex. 1*st*, line 1st, but heavier.

In line 7th, Ex. 1*st*, is condensed; Ex. 2*d*, shaded, and Ex. 3*d*, spurred.

(*n.*) After the systematic explanation of letter drawing, with varied illustrations, now given, the student should make an entire alphabet of each of the kinds of letters shown on Pl. VII.

(*o.*) In combining words to form the titles to maps and drawings, the most essential principles are the following.

1°. To vary the letters in size, or heaviness, or both, according to the relative importance of the different words of the title ; and the heaviness, or blackness, also, according to the general depth of color of the drawing.

2°. To make decided contrasts between the lengths of the different lines of lettering contained in the title, and so that the circumscribing figure, formed by joining the ends of the successive lines, shall have a pleasing outline.

When the spelling of the words makes this difficult, the use of "condensed," or "expanded" letters, or the prolongation of some of the lines of the title by long dashes, will afford considerable aid.

In connection with these principles, study the artistic features of titles, and title pages, critically, with a view to good typographical design.

(*p.*) In the old-fashioned styles of type recently revived, one of the most obvious marks of distinction is, that the arms of the E's, T's, etc., instead of being vertical, are divergent, as in the following letters.

E F H L T Z

(*q.*) Finally, remark (*i*) may be modified by adding that the arms should have vertical tangents, unless plainly meant not to have them, as if C, for example, in the first half of line 3*rd*, of Pl. VII., were to consist of three-fourths of a full circle.

PART II.

SOLID DRAWING.

CHAPTER I.

OBJECT, OR MODEL DRAWING.

§ 1.—Rectilinear Models.

Definitions and Principles.

THE angle made by two intersecting straight lines is called a *plane angle.*

The angular space enclosed by three or more plane surfaces which meet at a point, is called a *solid angle.* Thus the angle at one of the upper corners, B, of a room, see the figure, where two walls, ABD and CBD, and the ceiling ABC meet,

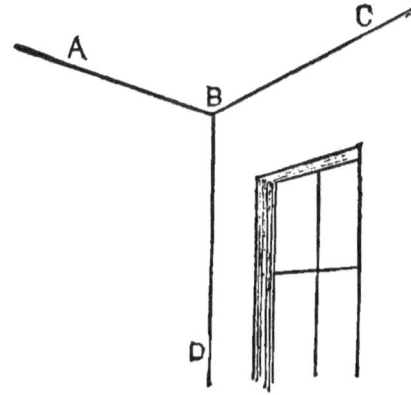

is a solid angle. In a square-cornered room, such an angle is a *solid right angle.* This is the simplest of solid angles, and is bounded by three plane right angles, one, ABC, in the ceiling formed by the meeting of two of its edges AB and

CB, and one in each of the connected walls, as ABD and CBD.

But there are many other solid angles, bounded by three or more plane angles, some or all of which may not be right angles. Thus the angle at the summit of any pyramid is a solid angle and is bounded by as many plane angles as the pyramid has sides.

These simple principles being apprehended, no large miscellaneous collection of models is necessary in order to obtain skill in making free-hand sketches of geometrical objects from the solids themselves. A few variously proportioned prisms and pyramids each placed in various positions, and singly, or combined, will afford an almost unlimited variety of practice in combinations of length and direction of straight lines. These objects can be made by any wood-worker, or by pupils for themselves, and may usefully be of wood or pasteboard; also skeleton forms may be made of wire or light wooden rods.*

A set of simple plane or flat-sided drawing models, of convenient size to be seen across a room, being provided, exercises upon them may be made *suitably progressive according to the three following principles.*

I. *Selecting for reference any one of the various solid angles of the body,* let the position of the body be taken, first, so as to show only one of its bounding plane angles; then two, and so on till the body shall be so placed as to show all the bounding plane angles of the given solid angle.

II. *Attending to the surfaces of the body,* let it first be placed so that but one such surface shall be visible, then two, and so on till the greatest possible number shall be visible.

III. For each position of the solid or closed model, place by the side of it, and in the same position, a *skeleton model of the same body,* which will further vary the exercise by showing lines that are hidden on the opaque model.

---

* When it is desired to purchase manufactured models, Harding's English models, architectural in character, and affording many combinations, may be found useful. So, also, will the excellent elementary sets manufactured at the Worcester (Mass.) Institute of Industrial Science, and which more closely agree with the principles here stated in the text. Other sets may perhaps be found on inquiry at Art, or School Supply stores.

PL.VI.

IHLFET·V
AKNMWZ
XY·JUDPB
RQCGS·&

PL. VII.

ABCDEFGHIJKLM   NOPQRSTUVWXYZ &

THE MODELS   **LOWER SURE**   *leaning*   MAIL STEAMER

ABCDEFGH IJKLMNO

PQRSTUVWXYZ

ABCDEFGHI JKLMNO

PQRSTU VWXYZ&A

PACKET COMPANY   HATCHER   HATCHER

bcdefghijkl mnopqrstuvwxyz *abcdefghijklmn*

Exercises.

Ex. 119, Pl. VIII., Fig. 1, represents a cube, selected for illustration, and placed so that but one face is seen.

Ex. 120, Fig. 2, represents the skeleton cube in the same position. All the edges will be visible, but in various ways, according as the eye of the observer is above or below, to the right or left of the position indicated by the figure, which is directly in front of E, the centre of the front of the cube.

Ex. 121. In Fig. 3, the eye is supposed to be above the level of the top of the cube, which is represented as turned so that three faces, c, m, and n, of the same solid angle are seen.

Ex. 122. Fig. 4 represents a similar position of the skeleton cube.

Ex. 123. Fig. 5 represents the cube as so related to the eye, that only c and n of the three angles shown in Fig. 3 are visible. The eye is here between the levels of the upper and lower bases of the cube.

Ex. 124. Fig. 6 represents the skeleton cube situated as in Fig. 5.

The pupil can easily satisfy himself by experiment that the nearer he approaches the cube, the more rapidly will the receding lines as $c\,d$ and $e\,f$, Fig. 3, appear to converge, and that the contrary result will take place, the further he removes from the object.

Exercises like the foregoing may be arranged for each of the elementary solids. Thus:

Ex. 125. Construct a series of six figures, of a solid, and of a skeleton triangular *pyramid*.

Ex. 126. Do. of a square pyramid.

Ex. 127. Do. of a hexagonal pyramid.

Ex. 128. Do. of an octagonal pyramid.

In each of these four exercises, it may be a solid angle at some corner of the base, or the one at the vertex which is chosen, for the purpose of guiding the changes of position of the pyramid. Thus, in the two following figures, Fig. 1 represents a square pyramid, in which three sides of the solid angle at a are visible. The pyramid is thus either supposed to be tipped backward so as to bring its base in sight; or else, if it stands on a level, to be above the level of the eye which may then be directly in front of some point as E. Fig. 2 represents a triangular pyramid, so placed that all of the plane angles at its vertex are visible.

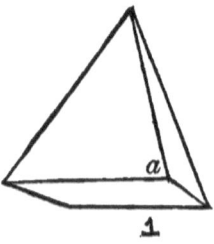
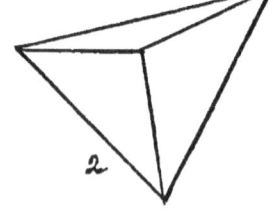

E⋅

Proceeding with these exercises:

Ex. 129. Draw six figures, three of a solid, and three of a skeleton triangular *prism*.

In this, and in each of the following exercises, the prism may be successively placed so as to show one, two, or all of the plane angles which bound some one of the solid angles at the *lower base;* or, to show the same for some one of the solid angles at the *upper base.*

Ex. 130. Draw, as above, a solid and a skeleton *square prism*, each in three or more successive positions of increasing complexity.

Ex. 131. Do the same with a *hexagonal prism*.

Ex. 132. Do the same with an *octagonal* prism.

§ 2.—Curvilinear Models.

The three elementary round bodies are the cylinder, the cone, and the sphere.

The sphere can never appear otherwise than circular, hence not much practice upon it is required, with respect to its *form;* though, in studying effects of *light* and *shade*, a series of varied exercises may be founded upon each body, by placing it in *the same position in various lights*, as well as in *different positions in the same light.*

The cylinder and cone can be placed in positions similar to those already described for the prism and pyramid. That is, with the upper base (or the vertex) inclined directly towards, or from the eye, inclined to the right or left or inclined diagonally forward or backward; that is to the north-east, south-east, north-west, or south-west, the observer facing the north.

Not more than half of the curved surface of a cylinder can be seen; but the entire convex surface of a cone can be made visible by inclining its vertex sufficiently towards the eye.

As the exercises proposed in this Second Part are intended to be drawn directly from objects conveniently placed before the eye, without the intervention of drawn or printed copies,* no engraved copies are here given; but the pupil should draw next, each of the three round bodies in various positions.

After sufficient practice in drawing single bodies, a final series of exercises should consist in drawing various combinations of them, the combinations consisting of different bodies of the same kind, as prisms; and then of bodies of different kinds, as, for example, a group consisting of a prism, a pyramid, a cone, and a sphere, resting upon each other.

---

* If, however, an intermediate stage of work be, in some cases, preferred, large line, or shaded copies of drawings of solids can doubtless be readily provided.

CHAPTER II.

PERSPECTIVE AND PROJECTION FREE-HAND DRAWING.

Definitions.

I. *A perspective drawing* is one which represents the object as it would appear when seen at ordinary distances. The most obvious and familiar characteristic of such drawings is, that lines in them, whose originals on the object are parallel, generally converge to a common point.

Thus, in looking down a long stretch of straight railroad track, or through a very long building, as a large freight depot, the rails in the one case, and the side walls in the other, appear to approach each other as they recede from the eye.

For this reason, a perspective drawing is in one sense a distorted representation of the object drawn. That is, it does not represent it as the object actually *is*, but only as it *appears*, when viewed from some given point. For instance, see the six figures of the cube on Pl. VIII., the necessary convergence of the receding lines distorts the angles, making those which in reality *are* all right angles, *appear* either as acute or obtuse angles, according to their position relative to the eye of the observer.

If, however, these oblique angles of the drawing impress the mind as being true representations of actual right angles on the object, this result is owing to the modifying effect of our intimate knowledge of the actual shape of the familiar object. But note, that this effect will not be produced, unless the picture and the object are both viewed similarly, in respect to distance and direction.

II. *Projection drawings.* When, however, the beholder is at a very great distance from the object, as compared with the dimensions of the latter, the lines which are parallel on the object, will be so on the drawing also. Drawings made under this supposition, viz., that the object is seen from an indefinitely great distance, are called *projection drawings*, or simply *projections*.

Both of the kinds of drawing just described, and whether made by the free hand or instrumentally, are of use to every one who has occasion to draw. Yet as *perspective drawings* represent objects only as they *appear*, they are chiefly of use to artists; in other words, to those who make pictures for our pleasure. But as *projection drawings* represent the forms of objects as they really *are*, they are more useful to industrial designers, in making patterns or copies, from which things to use are to be made.

Thus, of the two figures of a goblet, shown in Pl. VIII., Figs. 7 and 8, the first represents it as it might appear standing before one at the table, and is a *perspective view*. The second is a *projection drawing* of the same goblet, showing its height, and its diameters at several points on its centre line or axis, on a uniform scale of one third of the full size. The former is therefore merely *pictorial*, while the latter might guide a workman in making goblets of the particular pattern shown.

The final drawing to be strictly followed by the workman might be very accurately laid out by scale, of the full size of the goblet and drawn with instruments. But the preliminary drawings, to indicate the design and its effect, would be drawn by the free hand, whether in perspective, or projection, or both. Hence, as already explained in connection with other applications, the usefulness of the free-hand drawing of geometrical, as well as of natural objects.

Indicated Exercises. Properties and Treatment of Wood.

The following are some of the articles in the drawing of which the pupil can usefully exercise himself, and which each can generally find at hand in his home without the necessity of collecting models.

First, household wares.

Knives, forks, spoons, castors, tea sets, tubs, pumps, stoves, pitchers, bowls, cups, saucers, dishes, etc.

Second, furniture.

Under this head a qualifying remark is necessary. Wood may be treated in two radically different ways; *first*, independently of its nature as having generally, or, except in root, knot, or crotch pieces, an essentially straight grain ; *second*, with strict reference to its structure in this respect. These different ways give rise to two corresponding parties relative to ornamental design in wood. The one, treating it as if it were plastic, or like marble, without a fibrous grain, produces the kind of work often seen, abounding in curved outlines and carving, as seen in curved and carved table and piano legs (see the annexed figure), sofa and picture frames.

The other party claim that wood should be treated strictly according to its nature, that is in straight pieces running with the grain. Thus purely angular, not curved, geometrical work is produced, as seen very simply in the straight backed chairs of our grandfathers, and more elaborately in what is popularly known at present as the " Eastlake style."

So far, however, as some kinds of wood, as ash, and others, are capable, at least under certain treatment, of being very much and variously bent without breaking, as in the "Austrian bent wood" furniture, shown at the Centennial Exhibition, and in many of our light office arm-chairs, it may be fairly claimed that the design does no violence to the nature of the wood. Also, so far as woods can be found of so close and tenacious a grain, that the cutting of successive layers of grain, as in a tapering turned table leg, never has the effect of causing a splintering or peeling up of these layers where thus cut off,

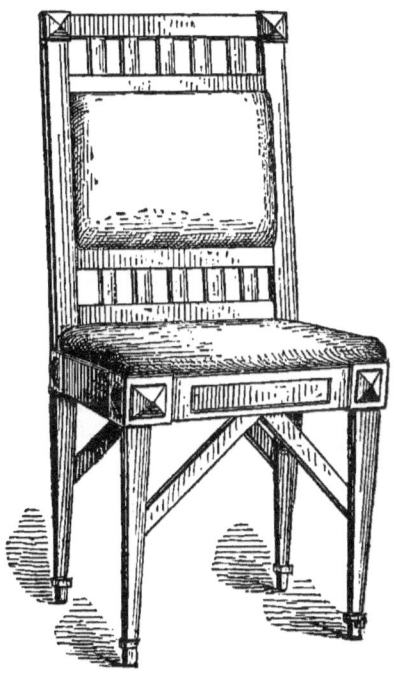

the wood seems to indicate, by its behavior, that no violence is done to its natural properties by curving, moulding, or carving it. From this point of view, the rigid exclusion of all but straight outlines and angularly geometrical forms from ornamental wood-work, would seem to be more of a fancy, than well-founded in principle.

With these explanations, the pupil will find frequent and useful examples for free-hand drawing of geometrical objects in articles of furniture having a regular geometrical form, such as Chests — Clocks—Work-boxes—Book-cases—Tables—Desks—Etc.

CHAPTER III.

PICTORIAL PROJECTION SKETCHING.

Definitions and Principles.

THERE are special kinds of projection drawing (Chap. II. II.) which combine the exactness of representation of projection drawing, with a good measure of the pictorial effect of perspective drawings (Chap. II. I.), especially as applied to small objects. They are therefore highly appropriate for the freehand sketching of such objects.

Without going into the principles and details of this subject here, enough will be explained by illustration, to enable the pupil, beginning by imitation of copies, to serve himself sufficiently until he studies the subject fully.*

In Pl. VIII., Figs. 9 to 14, illustrate these pictorial projections by the most elementary examples.

The two first, or Figs. 9 and 10, represent a cube already otherwise shown in Pl. VIII., Figs. 1 and 2.

Isometrical Drawing.

Here the first figure represents a solid cube, placed so that the three plane right angles, a, b, c, which unite to form the solid angle of the cube nearest the eye, are equally exposed, and hence appear of equal size. Hence this kind of drawing is called *isometrical drawing*, the name meaning *equal measure*. The second figure represents a skeleton cube of the same size as before. Owing to the entirely regular form of the cube, the equality of all its sides and angles, the most remote corner, at which the three edges, de, fg, hk, meet, appears to coincide with the nearest one, abc.

---

* See Isometrical Drawing, etc., in my "ELEMENTARY PROJECTION DRAWING."

PICTORIAL PROJECTION SKETCHING. 67

Ex. 133. Draw the cubes as here shown, but much larger. The angles at a, b, c, in the drawing, are equal, and of 120° each. The other angles are of 60°, or 120°, as shown.

Oblique Projection.—Again, instead of supposing the object to be directly in front of the eye, but inclined as just explained and illustrated, we may suppose the object to be above or below the eye, and also at the right or left of it. The object is also still supposed to be at so great a distance from the eye that its parallel lines will appear parallel. The four figures, 11 to 14, of Pl. VIII., illustrate this case, by the representation of a half cube seen in as many different directions. They are called *oblique projections* to distinguish them from the preceding, and because the supposed position of the body causes it to be viewed obliquely.

All lines in the isometrical figures, in other directions than those shown, would appear less than their real size, as in case of one from a to e, or greater, as one from d to g. The like is true of all lines in the oblique projections, except all lines in the front faces A, B, C, D; which show their real *form* as well as *dimensions*.

Ex. 134. Fig. 11, represents the half cube as seen from below and to the right. Draw also the whole cube.

Ex. 135. Fig. 12, the same as seen from below and to the left. Draw likewise any other square prism.

Ex. 136. Fig. 13, as seen from above and to the right of it. Draw also the whole cube.

Ex. 137. Fig. 14, as seen from above and to the left of it. In each case the line ac, on the body itself, is perpendicular to the front face of the body, and on the drawing, is made equal to $\frac{1}{2}$ ab.

The edges which are parallel to ac on the block itself, are parallel to ac in the drawing, on account of the supposed very great distance of the eye from the object, although they would appear to converge in a true perspective drawing (Chap. II. I.). Nevertheless, these figures, as well as the isometric ones, have a pictorial effect which makes them more intelligible to those workmen and others who have little familiarity with drawing, than ordinary projections are (Chap. II. II.); while they possess the practical advantage of showing the three dimensions of the object in their real size.

Practical Applications.

Suppose, now, that a person wishes to have made for him, a covered rectangular tank, with a raised square covered opening near one end. The figures, 1–4 of Pl. IX., afford a connected illustration of the kinds of drawing already explained.

Ex. 138. Fig. 1, is a *perspective view* of the tank, not showing any of its dimensions truly. To appear not distorted, the eye should be about four inches directly in front of a point a little above E.

Ex. 139. Fig. 2, shows a pair of *projections*, together representing all the dimensions on a uniform scale; the lower one, A, is a top view, called a *plan*, and shows the length and width of the tank; the upper one, B, is a front view, called the *elevation*, and shows the length and height.

Ex. 140. Fig. 3, is an isometrical figure, where all the angles are right angles on the object, but appear as angles of 60° or 120° in the drawing.

Ex. 141. Fig. 4, is an oblique projection of the same tank. Both of the last two figures have nearly as much of intelligible pictorial character as the first figure, with the added practical advantage of showing all the dimensions as truly as the projections in the second figure do, and more intelligibly to ordinary eyes.

The remaining figures of Pl. IX., show a variety of applications of the projections now explained.

Ex. 142. Fig. 5, shows a nut A, and bolt B. The nut is six-sided, and, according to the properties of a prism of six equal sides, the lateral faces, C and D, each appear just half as wide as the middle one. By experiment with a regular six-sided prism, the pupil can easily find how the nut would appear if only two of its faces were visible.

Ex. 143. Fig. 6, shows a partial plan, B, and elevation, A, of a square nut, the plan or top view being made first, its corners being, as shown by the dotted lines, a guide to the position of the vertical edges of the elevation.

Figs. 7 and 8 show how to make correct isometrical drawings of objects whose lines are not all at right angles to each other. These lines, as indicated by the faint lines and the letters, are located from lines parallel to those in Fig. 3, since only such lines show their real size.

Ex. 144. Fig. 7, represents a frustum of a square pyramid; drawn, as indicated, by inscribing it in a prism of the same base and altitude.

Ex. 145. Fig. 8, a fire-place. Draw Fig. 8 first as shown, and then with the longer edges, as MN, in the direction MO, which will bring the opposite end of the fire-place in sight.

Figs. 9, 10, 12, illustrate the isometric drawing of curved objects. Each face of a cube, Fig. 9, being a square, a circle can be inscribed in it, touching each side of the square at its middle point.

Ex. 146. Fig. 9 shows the appearance of the isometrical drawing of a cube with circles thus inscribed in its three visible faces. Note that the diameter of the circle is equal to the side of the circumscribing square.

Ex. 147. Fig. 10 shows a frustum of a cone, isometrically, its bases being drawn by means of their circumscribing squares which are placed in the same position as *abcd* in Fig. 9. The axis, MN, joining the centres, M and N, of the bases of the frustum, might have been in the direction of *cb*, Fig. 9. Then the circumscribing squares of the bases would have been in the position *cdef*, Fig. 9. MN could also have been in the direction of *cd*, Fig. 9, and these squares would then have had a position like *bceg* in that figure. The pupil should draw the frustum in the three positions here described.

Ex. 148. Fig. 12 is the isometrical drawing of a pipe with a flange at each end, the axis of the pipe being in the direction of *cd*, Fig. 9. According to the explanations just made, draw this pipe as it would appear with its axis lying in the direction *cb* or *ce*, Fig. 9.

Ex. 149. Finally, Fig. 11, is an *oblique projection* of a pipe similar to the last. The figure is more easily drawn, since the circular ends are circular in the figure.

Ex. 150–153. Draw Figs. 7, 8, 9, and 10 in oblique projection. By careful comparison of Figs. 5 to 12 with each other, and with 2, 3, 4 as standards, the pupil can learn to make plan and elevation, isometrical, and oblique projection sketches of many common objects; such as boxes with compartments, etc., etc.

At this point, the pupil can also profitably, with reference to the exercises to follow, practice the drawing of various curved objects in isometrical and oblique projection. Such objects may be a Cylinder, a Cone, the Frustum of a cone, Rings, both of square and circular cross-section, Vases, etc. These may be taken, first, separately, and then in combination; placing them first in the simplest positions, and thence advancing to more irregular positions.*

The drawings in these cases should be on plates twice as large as those of this book, and the models should be large, from ten to sixteen inches high.

Figs. 3 and 5, Pl. X., are examples of the application of oblique projection to the drawing of models of problems in space, either on the black-board, or for book illustration.

Ex. 154. Fig. 3 represents two planes, H, horizontal, and V, vertical, so placed that V is in the position of the front faces of the blocks shown in Pl. VIII., Figs. 11–14. ABC is then a square cornered block, whose front face is parallel to V, and top, ABD, parallel to H.

The figure abd, equal to ABD and directly under it, on H, is then called the "horizontal projection," or "*plan*" of the block.

Likewise the figure $a'b'c'$, equal to ABC, and directly behind it, on V, is called the "vertical projection," or "*elevation*" of the block. See Pl. IX., Fig. 2.

Ex. 155. Pl. X., Fig. 5, represents similar planes, H, and V, in the positions parallel to the right hand and top faces of the blocks, shown in Figs. 11 to 14 of Pl. IX., and viewed as indicated in Fig. 13. Then PQP' represents a plane, as of paper or tin, meeting H in the line ("trace") PQ, and meet-

---

* See note on p. 58.

ing V in the line P'Q. This plane is then pierced at O (whose projections on H and V are c and c') by the line AB, whose projections are ab and $a'b'$.

Figures like these are highly useful in representing combinations of forms in space, such as would not be so readily intelligible from ordinary diagrams. Most of the figures in "solid geometry" can advantageously be drawn in this way.

The remaining figures of Pl. X. give examples, but of details, only, and on a suitable scale for practice, of the *structure and machine sketching*, which is one of the several practical applications contemplated in the more elementary drill afforded in the earlier chapters of Part I.

Fig. 1, as indicated by the braces, shows three views of the assemblage of parts at one of the joints in the floor of a kind of bridge.

Ex. 156. The lower figure is a sketch, as seen in a side view of a bridge, of the structure of the floor at the point where one of the main cross-beams is suspended by iron rods, as R, from the supporting frame, or truss above. This beam is composed of the four pieces whose ends are shown. The lateral ones, A, B, bolted to the deeper central ones, form rests for the floor-joists, m, which lie lengthwise of the bridge and support the floor planks p. The irregular cast iron block below, is shaped with wings ($3'' \times 8''$) which support the iron links LL, which tie the bridge together like a bow-string; and form a bearing below for the nut on the lower end of the suspension rod R. Directly over this, the "plan" shows only the chain links L and the under side of the cast iron block, O.

At the right of the plan is shown the view of the several parts as seen in looking at the end of the bridge. This figure should be viewed, looking to the right, while facing the left hand end of the plate. The same parts bear the same letters in the three views embraced in the figure.

Views of different sides of the same thing should be drawn on the *same scale*, and placed on the *same level*, when not arranged as in Fig. 1. The eye can then pass readily from one view to the other, and trace the corresponding views of the same parts.

Ex. 157. Pl. X., Fig. 2 shows a method of firmly binding

together two timbers, M and N, at right angles, without cutting either of them. This is here done by harpoon bolts, one of which is A, A', where A' is a view at right angles to that shown at A, and shows that the upper end of the bolt is beaten out flat. The bolts pass through N, the hook hh' gives them a hold on M, which is secured by the small cross bolt, b.

Ex. 158. Pl. X., Fig. 4 shows a plan, or top view of a joint of the iron truss of the same bridge to which Fig. 1 belongs, and at the upper end of one of the rods, as R, Fig. 1.

Ex. 159. Fig. 6 shows the stout casting, called a *shoe*, which receives the ends of the last pair of tie rods, T, lying in the direction of LL, Fig. 1; also the foot of the iron truss.

Ex. 160. Fig. 7 is a plan and elevation of a "shaft coupling," or, one form of the many contrivances for locking together two pieces, A and B, of a line of shafting. In this example, this is done by means of a stout collar, C, in two pieces bolted together, and a key, k, partly let into the shafts and partly into the collar.

On the preceding figures, the measurements indicate by arrow-heads the distances or dimensions to which they refer, and denote feet by single accents, and inches by two accents. Thus, $3':6''$ is read, three feet and six inches.

Guided by these examples, the learner should exercise himself in making neat pencil sketches, after the manner of those on Plates IX. and X., but larger, of such mechanical objects as are accessible, such as railroad chairs, frogs, and switches; grindstones, hay-cutters, bridge joints; roof-framings, as found in barns, attics, etc.

These sketches should be large enough to exhibit the smallest parts, and contain the recorded measurements without confusion, or obscurity.

By practice in thus *carefully sketching*, and neatly and completely measuring the parts of any structures accessible to him, of wood or iron, or masonry work, or machines, or parts of them, the learner will not only learn to make such sketches readily and neatly, which will often be a serviceable accomplishment, but will, by degrees, collect an album of valuable examples of construction, the exact knowledge of which may be useful.

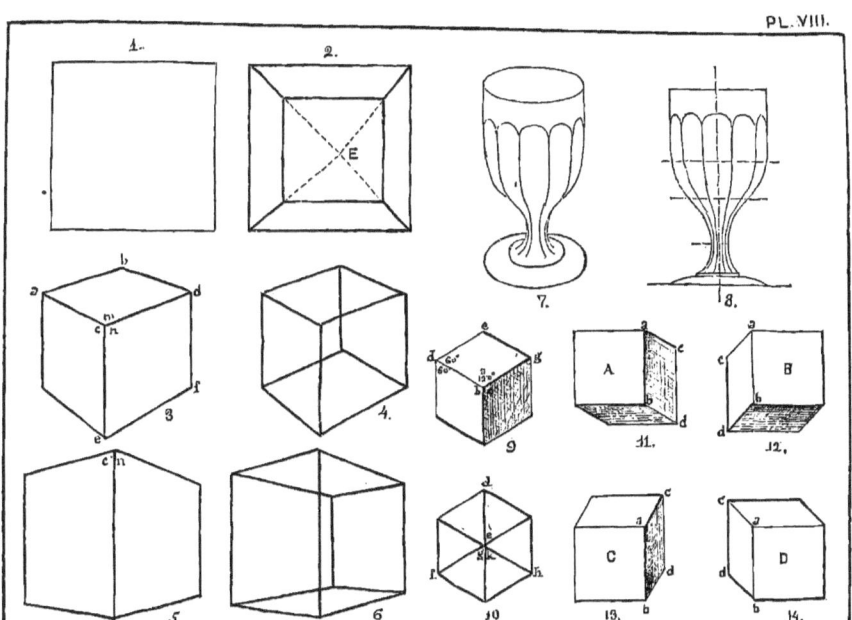

PL. VIII.

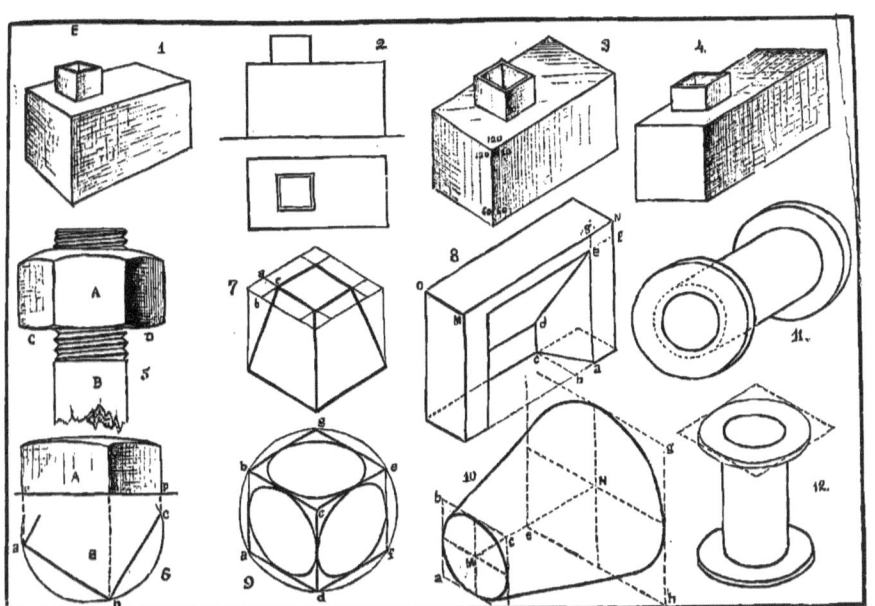

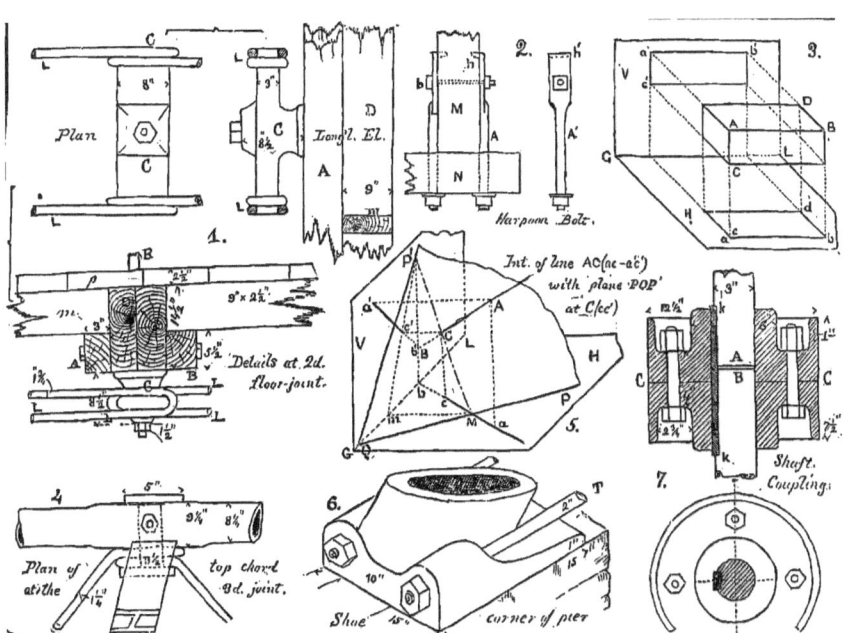

PART III.

ELEMENTS OF GEOMETRIC BEAUTY.

CHAPTER I.

ELEMENTARY IDEAS. UNITY, VARIETY, FREEDOM.

1. The human mind everywhere contains among its possessions, the idea of *beauty*.

Thus, it is familiar to every one that there are a multitude of objects which give us great pleasure, independently of any practical use that they have. That quality of objects, by reason of which they afford this pleasure, is called their *beauty*.

2. It may not be possible yet to give a definition of beauty that shall include every possible case. But it seems highly probable that it consists in *expressiveness of good*, where GOOD is defined as perfection of structure, or *being ;* of action, or *doing ;* and of consequent acquisition, possession, or *having*.

3. *Examples.*—The beauty of a goblet, as distinguished from a tin cup—though the latter, being more durable and capable of many more uses, has far more *utility*—lies in part in its expressiveness of the fitness of things, which is a kind of good. That is, water being transparent and colorless, yet sparkling, there is beauty in the idea of drinking it from a material like itself in these respects, from a vessel which seems as if made of water that had become permanently solid.

Again, the beauty of a statue of perfect youth, so life-like that it makes even marble seem flexible, consists in its clear expressiveness of the suppleness, readiness, abounding life, and varied capability which are so many perfections of being. Also, in its expressiveness of the mastery of mind over matter, shown in the genius of the sculptor.

Once more, the beauty of a greyhound consists in the evident expressiveness, in every line and conformation of his body, of the word, "go," whispered in his ear at his creation, as seen in the evident delight with which he runs a race with every fleet horse that passes his gate.

4. But *there are many orders of beauty*, corresponding to as many departments of thought. One of these relates to beauty of *form*.

Beauty of form is of two kinds; the one free, flexible, mobile; the other rigid, precise, fixed. The beauty of a flower, or a statue, is of the former kind; that of a building or a pavement of geometrical inlaid work, is of the latter kind.

A statue is placed under the first head, not because *it* is flexible, but because it represents flexible beauty, and, in proportion to its perfection, represents it so perfectly as to seem flexible; so that the climax of the sculptor's art lies in such completeness of triumph of mind over matter as to make rigid material seem flexible.

5. Of these two species of beauty, one, as we have said, relates to regular, or as it may therefore be called, *geometric beauty*.

This alone concerns us now, as appropriately connected with a course of *free-hand geometrical* drawing, auxiliary to a course of *instrumental* geometrical drawing.

Now the exactness of everything geometrical renders it certain that, if definite principles and resulting rules can be found anywhere, by following which beautiful forms can certainly be produced, it will be in the department of geometric beauty.

There is reason to suppose that the ancient Greeks possessed and used such rules, unless their marvellous genius for such beauty, as well as for purely free or non-geometrical beauty, made them infallibly, though unconsciously, conform to them.

6. Let us next examine this idea of *beauty* and seek to find some of its parts or elements.

Unity.—Passing by a large vacant city lot at a certain time, we may notice in process of collection a large amount of scattered stone—iron—lumber—lime.

Passing the same spot a year or two later, we find that all

these materials, with other finer ones, have been combined to form a grand temple of art, science, or religion.

The human mind, of itself, feels and knows a difference between these two cases, and expresses the difference in appropriate speech.

The first is an assemblage of materials for a purpose not yet realized. This assemblage is, to the mind, no one thing, and takes no distinctive name as any one thing.

The finished building embraces the same materials, but combined for *one purpose*. This one purpose, governs the orderly arrangement of the before scattered materials, and makes each piece contribute in some way towards the fulfilment of that purpose. This fact makes the result one thing to the mind, to which one name can therefore be given—a museum, or a church.

Hence we say, that *unity* is one of the primary ideas of the human mind, and that a principle of unity pervades and binds together things otherwise thought of as separate.

7. *Illustrations.*—It is this same idea which makes the difference between anarchy and civil order; between chaos and creation, and which makes the mind always conceive of the sum of all things as being really one thing, because the product of one mind, for some one all-embracing purpose, and hence called the *universe.*

Finally, there is no stronger proof of the permanent reality of this idea of unity, than the existence, always and everywhere, of systems of philosophy. For philosophy, as is plain from many definitions of it, is an attempt to discover the central or initial thought, purpose, or idea, from which all things visible and invisible spring. In other words, it is an attempt to see the universe as from its centre; in a word, to place ourselves in the *position* of Deity, with the *intelligence* of Deity—as Plato said 2,000 years ago, " a resembling of the Deity so far as that is possible to man."

8. *Kinds of Unity. Uniformity.*—But UNITY is of two kinds, *simple* and *compound*. To continue a former illustration, one brick, one board, in the building is a simple unit, as being of uniform substance throughout, and not formed by putting together separate pieces. On the other hand, the entire building is a unit, because made for one purpose, and *evidently*

made for one purpose, in that every part of it contributes towards the attainment of that one purpose. Yet it is a highly compound unit, because composed of many separate parts.

When the separate parts are like the whole, or when, if the nature of the case renders this impossible, the like components are equal and similarly placed, the principle of *uniformity* enters, and the unity, though still compound, is simplified, or more nearly approaches simple unity.

Hence we have not only unity, but *unity in variety*, with, or without *uniformity* also, as an element in the idea of beauty. As each part co-operates with the others to form the unity of the whole, we will call this compound unity, *harmony*.

9. *Freedom.*—But there is variety in a higher sense. There may be twenty great buildings all built for the same purpose. Yet they may all be well adapted to that purpose and hence beautiful, though built in twenty different ways, or from the plans of twenty different designers, none of whom ever saw the plans of any of the others.

This kind of variety may be a part of what is meant when writers on Art speak of the "freedom of the domain of art" as compared with the precise rules by which we are bound in mathematical operations; and when they speak of the freedom of the mind over matter, when the mind seeks to express its ideas and purposes by material forms.

This variety indicates the principle of *freedom*, since it results from such action as is most unconscious of conformity to rules, and is most difficult, if not impossible, to bring under the operation of rules.

10. *Primary relation of fundamental proportions to accessories.*—In analyzing the variety just described, nothing is more familiar than the habit of distinguishing between the *proportions* and the *decorations* of a structure. And no principle is, or should be, more familiar than that no kind or amount of decoration can conceal or compensate for deformity of the naked proportions, skeleton, or framework, which supports those decorations.

Now the very *idea* of proportions, is, that they are something of a definite geometrical character, having precisely measurable, or numerical relations between them. This being true, it follows that the skeleton—that is, the figure composed of the principal lines of any structure, or other object, should form a geometrical figure governed by the laws of agreeable geometrical proportion; supposing, as in Art. 4, that it is possible to discover these laws.

11. *Summary.*—We are now prepared to enter upon the study of geometrical beauty, guided by the three principles of *Unity; Harmony;* and *Freedom,* such as may be exercised upon an *underlying frame or skeleton having beautiful geometrical proportions.*

These terms, harmony and freedom, are not inconsistent, as should here be understood, with the terms, symmetry and combination, before used (see Part I., Chap. VII.); for symmetry is but one species of harmony, and freedom consists partly in the multitude of combinations which can be made from the same elements.

CHAPTER II.

NUMERICAL EXPRESSION OF THE ELEMENTARY IDEAS.

12. VITRUVIUS is the one ancient writer on architecture and its details, to whom modern writers refer; and his knowledge of the principles of Greek art seems to have been traditionary and incomplete. Yet he says, "The several parts which constitute a temple ought to be subject to the *laws of symmetry;* the *principles* of which ought to be familiar to all who profess the science of architecture. *Proportion* is the commensuration of the various constituent parts with the whole, in which symmetry consists."[1] And he then describes the details of the proportions of the human body, as being the most beautiful created thing; and says "the laws of symmetry were derived by the artists of antiquity" (the Greeks of whom he wrote) "from the proportions of the human body."

13. But how these laws of symmetry were derived from the human body he does not show.

Nevertheless we have the following clue to their possible discovery.

1°. The eye and the ear are sometimes spoken of as the nobler senses, the especial senses of the soul.

2°. There are accordingly provided, to satisfy these senses, *beauty of sound for the ear*, and *beauty of form for the eye*.

3°. The laws of concordant sounds, harmonious to the ear, are well known. If then, taking the human body as an illustration of the utmost beauty of form, its proportions should be found subject to the same laws as those of harmonious sounds, the principles of unity and harmony already explained would make it seem highly probable, that the true principles of exact or *geometric* beauty of *form* were the same as those of exact or *harmonic* beauty of sound. For, moreover, the principle of *freedom*, as well as of mathematical precision, enters the domain of both eye and ear. This is seen in the beauty of oratory and elocution, as distinguished from music, properly so called, which corresponds, it may be, with the beauty of natural objects as distinguished from geometrical ones; or more exactly, in the fact that various pieces of music may yet be, in some evident manner, appropriate to the same words.

14. *Direction, the primary element of Form.*—The two elements of form are direction and length. The following considerations seem to show that direction is the more fundamental of these.

First, practical considerations. If the inquiries of a hundred *travellers* seeking their way to an unknown location were noted, it would probably be found that they would ask "which way," before they asked "how far."

Again in describing a *survey*, it has long been customary to describe the direction, called the bearing, of each line, before stating its length.

Once more, in making any *ornamental design*, whether of regular or free outline—but especially in the latter case, as in sketching fruit and flower forms or scroll work—the mind is more occupied with the *direction* to be given to the pencil at each point of its progress, than to the *size* of the sketch to be produced.

Second. But a precise geometrical reason may be found in the fact, that the triangle, the fundamental figure into which all others may be decomposed, may have an infinity of sizes, all of one shape, but cannot have any variety of form with a fixed length for each side.

That is, in similar triangles, similarly placed, the corresponding sides may be of different length, but have the same direction.

15. It may be objected that there can be many triangles of the same size or area, but of different forms, as well as many of the same forms but of different sizes, and thus that the ideas of direction of sides, and length of sides are equally fundamental. But it is to be noticed that the similar forms of different sizes can be instantly perceived to be similar, while the equal sizes, of different forms, could only be known to be equal, by measurement and computation of their areas.

Also, if one were trying to sketch a symmetrical, that is an isosceles triangle of pleasing form, he would do it by trying various angles between the base and the adjacent sides, as indicated at A, Fig. 1, until he found a triangle of pleasing proportions; rather than by trying various given lengths, as *c* and *d*, of those sides, placing them together by means of dividers, as indicated at BC and BD.

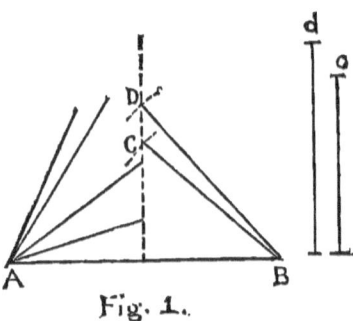

Fig. 1.

16. *Summary.*—*Distance* and *Direction*, are two radical geometrical ideas. *Distance* lies at the foundation of *size*, as large or small. *Direction* lies at the foundation of *form*, or the shape of things; and it is the form of objects rather than their size, which determines their beauty. Hence direction appears as the root idea in geometrical forms.

17. *An angle* is difference of direction, or the measure of relative direction. Hence it seems natural to look for the principles of geometric beauty in the *ratios between the angles* of figures, rather than in those between the lengths of their sides.

Some remarkable numerical properties of the circle, as the measure of angles at its centre, will confirm this view.

18. The circle has for ages been divided into 360 equal parts, called degrees, for the purposes of angular measurement. Whether the selection of this number was the result of accident, or experiment, or of abstract reasoning, may not now be known; but its relation to the principles of unity, variety, and harmony, as expressed by numbers, is very striking.

First. Its prime factors are

1. 2. 2. 2. 3. 3. 5 = 360. Now,

1°. These factors are the abstract unit, 1, and its *first three prime multiples*.

2°. Of these factors, 2, the *first even number*, consists of the two equal halves 1 and 1. It is therefore expressive of the principle of *uniformity*, as in the division of a body into two equal halves.

3°. Next, 3, is the *first odd number*. It can be separated only into the equal parts 1, 1, 1, or the unequal ones 1 and 2. It is thus the first and simplest numerical representative of the principle of *variety*.

4°. Next, 5, is the second simple or prime multiple of 1, and the first and simplest which combines in itself the numerical representatives of uniformity and variety, 2, and 3. It is therefore the simplest numerical representative of the combination of *uniformity with variety*.

19. The factor 2 is the foundation of the series 2, 4, 6, 8, etc., made by taking 1, 2, 3, etc., successively as multipliers. The factor 3 is likewise the foundation of the series 3, 6, 9, 12, etc.; and 5, is likewise the first term of the series 5, 10, 15, etc.

The numbers afforded by these series can, however, be better exhibited with regard to the details of their dependence on the primary numbers 2, 3, 5, as follows, where the exponent of each primary number is the multiplier for the series begun by that number.

2^2, 4, 8, 16, etc.
2^3, 6, 18, etc.
2^5, 10, 25, etc.
3^2, 6, 12, etc.
3^3, 9, 27, etc.
3^5, 15, 75, etc.
5^2, 10, 20, etc.
5^3, 15, 45, etc.
5^5, 25, 125, etc.

20. The factors of 360, properly combined by multiplication, yield all of the nine digits except 7, viz., 1; 2; 3; $2 \times 2 = 4$; 5; $2 \times 3 = 6$; $2 \times 2 \times 2 = 8$; $3 \times 3 = 9$.

The same numbers are also found in the foregoing series. But seven is peculiar, in containing none of the radical numbers 2, 3, 5, as a factor, and as a sum, $3+2+2$, it is redundant as compared with 5, in containing 2, twice. To be sure, 8 as a sum, $2+3+3$ is redundant, though differently, but can be resolved into 2's, it being $2 \times 2 \times 2$, as 9 can into 3's, while 7 is impracticable.

4*

We conclude therefore that 2, 3, 5, are the primary numerical representatives of uniformity and variety, and of their combination without superfluity; and thence that 360 may have been chosen to express the divisions of a circle on account of its containing all the digits but 7.*

21. It is interesting to note in passing, that the remaining digit, 6, is the *first perfect number*, that is, one which is equal both to the *sum*, and to the *product*, $1+2+3$, and $1 \times 2 \times 3$, of its factors, and thus numerically represents, both as a sum and a product, the principles of unity, uniformity and variety and their combination.

22. Having thus arrived at the significance of the numbers 2, 3 and 5, the number of ways and the manner in which 360 contains them is quite surprising, as is distinctly shown to the eye, in the annexed table.

$$\begin{cases} 360 = 2 \times 2 \times 2 \times 45. & (1) \\ 360 = 3 \times 3 \ldots \times 40. & (2) \\ 360 = 5 \ldots \ldots \times 72. & (3) \end{cases}$$

$$\begin{cases} 72 = 2 \times 2 \times 2 \times 9. & (3) \\ 45 = 3 \times 3 \ldots \times 5. & (1) \\ 40 = 5 \ldots \ldots \times 8. & (2) \end{cases}$$

$$\begin{cases} 8 = 2 \times 2 \times 2 \times 1. & (2) \\ 9 = 3 \times 3 \ldots \times 1. & (3) \\ 5 = 5 \ldots \ldots \times 1. & (1) \end{cases}$$

That is: *First*, 360 contains, as before seen, 2 thrice as a factor; 3, twice and 5 once, with quotients, after successively dividing out all these factors, of 45, 40, and 72, in the three cases respectively. *Second*, these quotients contain the same factors in like manner, as shown in the second group. *Third*, the like is true again, taking the quotients of the second group in the order seen in the third group, where the final quotients are each, 1.

In this curious result, we see again, exhibited in numbers, the *principle of uniformity*.

But the order in which the first two groups of quotients are used as the next dividends, is found as indicated by the paren-

---

* The number 7 is also excluded generally in the formation of musical ratios, but is said to be employed in Chinese music, and it enters into the composition of some peculiar theoretical systems, not in actual use.

theses and the adjoining circle, by combining 1, 2, 3 in every possible order taken in rotation, in the direction of the arrow. Here again we have likewise the *principle of variety*.

23. *Ratio the principle of combination.*—Numbers can be compared in two ways, by *difference* and by *ratio;* difference being obtained by subtracting one number from another; and *ratio*, by dividing one by the other. Aristotle (as quoted by Hay) defines harmony as "the union of contrary principles" (as those of uniformity and variety) "having a *ratio* to each other." In beautiful *forms, proportions* constitute harmony; and Vitruvius defines harmony as "the *commensuration* of the various constituent parts with the whole;" that is, each part bears a certain *ratio* to the whole.

24. *The reason why ratio, rather than difference*, should be the combining principle of parts into a whole, seems to be that *difference* belongs to the domain of *things*, and *ratio*, to that of pure thought. That is, this is so in this sense, that things of a kind can be added or subtracted forming a greater or less number of things of the same kind, as 5 pounds + 3 pounds are 8 pounds; 10 feet − 2 feet are 8 feet, etc., processes which seem to imply after-thought, or the putting together, or putting apart of things complete in themselves.

But, on the other hand, we cannot multiply 5 pounds by 3 pounds, or divide 10 feet by 2 feet, and get any real result. We can however multiply 5 pounds by the abstract number, 3, giving 15 pounds, and divide 10 feet by the abstract number, 2, giving 5 feet.

Addition thus seems related to the miscellaneous assembling of the materials supposed in Art. 6, but *ratio* to their combination, primarily in the mind, and then realized by the hands, in a *thought-out system*, which is a unity, and not an assemblage; though a compound unit, in which however each component contributes in its proper degree to the intended use of the whole, as when the windows of a building are sufficient for its light, and its entrance doors sufficient for ingress and egress.

CHAPTER III.

GENERAL APPLICATIONS OF THE IDEA OF BEAUTY IN RATIOS.

Analogy of Form and Sound.

25. *Linear and superficial beauty.* Since ratios, rather than differences, determine harmonious proportions, beauty arising from marked divisions of a line, will consist in ratios between the parts of the line, or between the parts and the whole; ratios which, according to the last chapter, are derived from the numbers 1, 2, 3 and 5. Such ratios will be furnished to any desired extent by the several series given in Art. 19.

Again, coupling the principle of ratios, with that of direction, as more fundamental than distance, the *ratios between the angles* of a plane figure would determine the beauty of its proportions, rather than the ratios between the lengths of its sides. It only remains then to determine the natural unit of angular measure.

26. *The angular unit.* This unit must be simply an angle that is naturally, not arbitrarily fixed. Recurring then to the figures in Part I., Chapter II., p. 7, we see that when hg is moved either way from its position perpendicular to mk, the angle on one side of it is acute, and that on the other, obtuse. Acute angles may vary in size, infinitely between 0° and 90°, and obtuse angles may vary indefinitely between 90° and 180°. But the equal angles of 90° on each side of hg, when it is perpendicular to mk, are the limit between all acute and all obtuse angles. That is, the right angle, being of necessarily fixed size, is the standard of comparison for all other angles.

27. Beginning now with known principles, from which to proceed to the unknown, the first illustration of beauty sensibly derived from the divisions of a line, shall be the beauty of

GENERAL APPLICATIONS OF THE IDEA OF BEAUTY IN RATIOS. 85

sound, occasioned by the notes given out by the divisions of a vibrating string.

By showing that the long and well established laws of *musical* harmony, or beauty of *sound*, are based upon the numbers 2, 3, 5, and their multiples, it will be more readily apparent that the abstract principles of beauty already described in connection with these numbers, are also as truly the bases of *geometrical* harmony, or beauty of geometrical *form*.

That the musical terms employed may be better understood, a sketch of a portion of a piano or organ keyboard is here given. Fig 2.

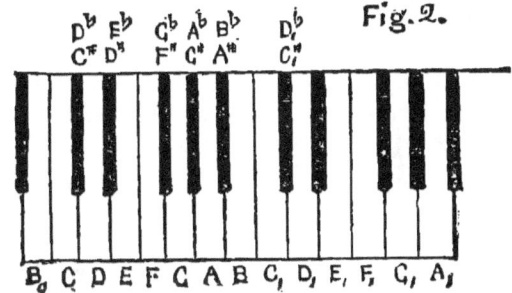

28. A note occasioned by a certain number of vibrations per second (fixed upon by agreement), whether of a stretched string, as in a viol, harp, or piano, or of a column of air, as in an organ pipe, is adopted as a standard of comparison, and designated by the letter C. A string *one-half* as long, Fig. 3, vibrates *twice* as fast, and gives a note designated as $C_{,}$, which is described as an *octave* above C. In other words, the difference in sound between these notes is called the *interval* of an octave.

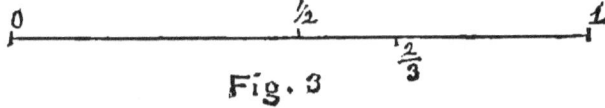

Again : $\frac{2}{3}$ of the length of the string will vibrate *three times* while the whole string vibrates *twice*, that is $\frac{3}{2}$ times while the whole string vibrates *once*, and will yield the note designated as G, and described as being at an *interval* of *a fifth* above C.

29. By continuing to take different simple fractional parts

of the string, based, according to preceding principles, on the numbers 2, 3, 5 and their multiples, we find the results given in the following table.

The *first* column contains the order of the notes and the letters which designate them; the *second*, the number of vibrations made in producing each note, during *one* of the vibrations made in producing *the note C;* the *third*, the number of vibrations made in producing each note, beginning with D, during one of the vibrations belonging to the *next preceding note ;* the *fourth*, the name of the *interval* between *each note and the first ;* the *fifth*, the name of the interval between each note after the first and the next preceding, these intervals being those which are expressed numerically by the ratios of the second and third columns respectively. The ratios in the *second* column are obtained experimentally. Those in the *third* are found as follows. Taking for illustration G and A, if we call $\frac{3}{2}=1$, what would $\frac{5}{3}$ become? Ans. $\frac{3}{2} : 1 :: \frac{5}{3} : \frac{1 \times \frac{5}{3}}{\frac{3}{2}} = \frac{2}{3} \times \frac{5}{3} = \frac{10}{9}$.

I.	II.	III.	IV	V.
1. C	1	1	1st.	1st, or unison.
2. D	$\frac{9}{8}$	$\frac{9}{8}$	2d.	Major 2d.
3. E	$\frac{5}{4}$	$\frac{10}{9}$	3d.	Minor 2d.
4. F	$\frac{4}{3}$	$\frac{16}{15}$	4th.	Diatonic semi-tone.
5. G	$\frac{3}{2}$	$\frac{9}{8}$	5th.	Major 2d.
6. A	$\frac{5}{3}$	$\frac{10}{9}$	6th.	Minor 2d.
7. B	$\frac{15}{8}$	$\frac{9}{8}$	7th.	Major 2d.
8. C$_1$	2	$\frac{16}{15}$	8th.	Diatonic semi-tone.

30. *Illustration of further application of ratios*, founded directly or indirectly on the primary numbers 2, 3, 5.

The intervals from C to E, from F to A, and from G to B each consisting of a major and a minor 2d—and $= \frac{5}{4}$—are called *major thirds*. Those from E to G, from A to C, and from B to the next higher D, each consist of a major 2d, and a diatonic semi-tone, and are each $= \frac{6}{5}$. Thus G, $\frac{3}{2} \div$ E, $\frac{5}{4} = \frac{3}{2} \times \frac{4}{5} = \frac{6}{5}$. These intervals are called *minor thirds*. Again, $\frac{5}{4} \div \frac{6}{5} = \frac{25}{24}$, an interval called a *chromatic semi-tone*.

Once more, F, $\frac{4}{3} \div$ D, $\frac{9}{8} = \frac{4}{3} \times \frac{8}{9} = \frac{32}{27}$ and $\frac{32}{27} \div \frac{6}{5} = \frac{32}{27} \times \frac{5}{6} = \frac{160}{162} = \frac{80}{81}$.

GENERAL APPLICATIONS OF THE IDEA OF BEAUTY IN RATIOS. 87

Also, $\frac{9}{8} : 1 :: \frac{10}{9} : \frac{10}{9} \div \frac{9}{8} = \frac{10}{9} \times \frac{8}{9} = \frac{80}{81}$. This interval, $\frac{80}{81}$, between the odd interval (D—F) and a minor third, or between a major and a minor 2d (remembering that $\frac{80}{81}$ means 80 vibrations belonging to one note, simultaneously with 81 vibrations belonging to another note) is called a *comma*.

31. *Sharps and Flats.*—A note so much *higher* than a given note that 25 of the vibrations which make it take place while 24 of those which make the given note occur, is called the *sharp* of that note, and is marked ♯. Also a note so much *lower* than a given note that 24 of the vibrations which make it occur during every 25 of those which make the given note, is called the *flat* of that note, and is marked ♭.

Thus we have,

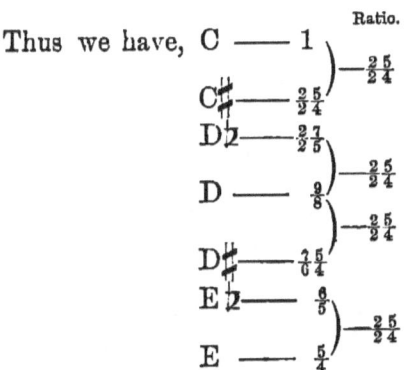

Continuing this process for every note of the scale, we shall find, in place of the eight notes, C to C_1 inclusive, twenty-one notes, with an exceedingly complicated variety of intervals, arising from the various combinations of major and minor tones and the diatonic and chromatic semi-tones.

32. *Keys and their mutual adjustment.*—No absolute note, that is, a note made by no fixed number of vibrations per second, need be taken as 1 of the musical scale. Any of the 21 tones just mentioned, may be taken as the initial note, called *the key note* of a scale in which the *order and value of the intervals shall be the same as in the scale just explained*, in which C is made 1 of the scale. But in any such new scale, a greater or less number of the notes will not coincide with some of the 21 notes of the complete scale which begins with C. Thus, a further and greater complication arises, out of the difference between the two kinds of tones and semi-tones already described.

A single illustration will suffice.

33. Suppose the note G to be assumed as 1 of a new scale. Such a scale is said to be in the *key of* G.

C
D
E
F
G—G, 1.
A—A′, 2. a comma higher than A, to give a major second as there should be (Art. 29) from 1 to 2 of the new scale (Art. 32).
B—B, 3. Minor second above A′.
C_1—C_1, 4. Diatonic semi-tone above B.
D_1—D_1, 5. Major 2d above C.
E_1—E_1, 6. Minor 2d above D.
F_1—F_1', 7. Major 2d above E_1.
G_1—G_1, 8. Diatonic semi-tone above F_1'.

It here appears that in the simple diatonic scale of eight tones, two new ones, a new A, called A′ and $\frac{81}{80}$, or a comma, above the A of the C scale, and a new F as described, are necessary to make the intervals exactly the same in the scales beginning with C, and G, respectively. And it will be found that two additional notes will be required to perfect each new scale; and more still would be required, if the semi-tones (sharps and flats) were all considered. But the intervals, very nearly $\frac{32}{31}$ between C$\sharp$ and D$\flat$ for instance, are so small, and especially so very small between either and a note which would be the mean between them, that it is usual to abolish the distinction between the sharps and flats of consecutive notes, thus for instance making C$\sharp$ and D$\flat$ identical, and also to abolish E$\sharp$, F$\flat$, B$\sharp$ and C$\flat$; all which abridgment reduces the 22 tones to 12, as shown in Fig. 2.

But with two additional tones for each new key note, an organ giving perfect intervals in the simple diatonic scale of eight notes, in eight keys, or scales, besides the C scale, would require $12, +8 \times 2 = 12 + 16 = 28$ pipes for every twelve now used. Such an instrument, though once, at least, actually built, would be extremely bulky; and in practice, the octave C to C_1 is divided usually into 12 *equal* intervals, thus rendering all scales alike, by making all equally imperfect.

34. *Temperament.*—The adjustment just described is called temperament, and may be broadly defined as *the limitation of free conformity to an ideal standard, in obedience to constraining conditions.* Thus, music performed on stringed instruments, like violins or harps, may be in perfect harmony in all keys, since the length of string necessary to produce any desired note may be regulated by the fingers. But with instruments with fixed keys, as for example, those having a piano key-board, it is nearly if not quite impossible to arrange more than twelve keys to the octave, though attempts have been made, by dividing the black keys, for example, to distinguish between the sharps and the flats of the principal notes. That is, the harmony is constrained by the mechanical difficulties of the problem, either relative to a practicable key-board, or to the bulkiness already explained in the last article.

Curious examples of temperament, as here defined, and analogous with musical temperament, will be found in connection with geometrical beauty.*

35. *Passing now from sound to form*, based on linear beauty, the following, a few among many of the linear proportions of the human form, remarkably coincide with the ratios existing between the vibrations in a given time, which produce harmonious sounds.

		Parts of the total height
From the sole of the foot to the	groin	$\frac{1}{2}$
" " " " "	5th or last vertebra of the loins	$\frac{3}{5}$
" " " " "	top of the hip bone	$\frac{4}{6}$
" " " " "	breast bone	$\frac{5}{6}$
" " " " "	bottom of the jaw bone	$\frac{7}{8}$
" " " " "	top " " "	$\frac{8}{9}$
" " " " "	base of the spine	$\frac{8}{10}$
From the base of the knee-pan to the top of the head		$\frac{3}{4}$

---

* It is of course not indispensable that the theory of music, even only so far as is here indicated, should be understood in order to render the succeeding principles of geometric beauty intelligible, since each rests independently on the abstract principles of beauty founded, as before shown, on the numbers 2, 3, and 5. Only, if it be plainly seen, that musical harmony is expressed by ratios founded on these numbers, it will more readily appear that geometric beauty may be similarly founded.

CHAPTER IV.

APPLICATION TO TRIANGLES AND RECTANGLES.

Triangles.

36. *Proceeding from linear to superficial beauty*, and bearing in mind the principle of Arts. (16) and (17) we shall find its simplest geometrical expression in triangular figures whose *angles* have simple ratios to each other, founded on the numbers 2, 3, 5. And, of these triangles, right angle ones are the simplest in relation to our present subject, since they contain in themselves the standard angle of comparison for the other two angles. (26)

Formal beauty, thus founded upon the numbers 2, 3, 5, may be said to be of the first, second and third orders respectively.

37. The *simplest geometric beauty* of *the first order* will be represented by the isosceles right-angled triangle, Fig. 4, in

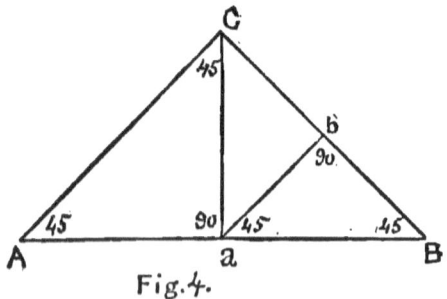

Fig. 4.

which the equal acute angles are to each other as 1 : 1, and to the right angle, as 1 : 2. Also this triangle can, as shown at A *a* C and *a b* B, be indefinitely divided into triangles similar to the whole one, ABC. It thus geometrically represents the principle of *uniformity*.

38. The simplest geometric beauty of the *second order* is

that of the equilateral triangle. For such a triangle, ABC, Fig. 5, is divided by its altitude CD into right angled triangles of 30°, 60°, 90°, giving the ratios ½, ⅓, ⅔, thus illustrating, by its exhibition of the number 3, in connection with 2, the first principle of *variety*.

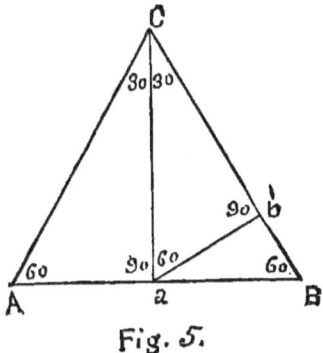

Fig. 5.

39. The simplest geometric beauty of the *third order* is that of the isosceles triangle having an angle of 36° and two of 72°, Fig. 6. For its altitude, CD, divides it into triangles of 18°, 72°, 90°, which exhibit the ratios ¼, ⅕, ⅘, thus, by including

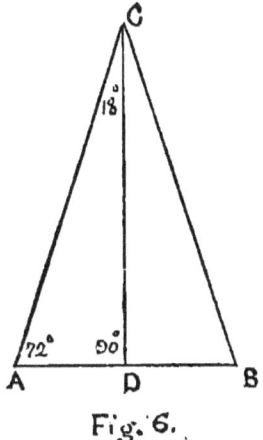

Fig. 6.

two ratios based on the number 5, illustrating the second principle of variety, the combination of uniformity with variety (Art. 18). It also, in the whole triangle, 36°, 72°, exhibits the ratio, ½.

40. *Derived ratios.* But from the *first* example (Art. 37) $\frac{1}{2}$, the ratio of 45° to 90°, is equal to the product, $\frac{2}{3} \times \frac{3}{4}$, where $\frac{2}{3}$ may be the ratio of 30° to 45°, of 45° to 67° : 30′ and 60° to 90°; and where $\frac{3}{4}$ may be the ratio of 67° : 30 to 90°. Thus is derived a harmonic triangle of 22° : 30′; 67° : 30′; 90°, giving ratios of $\frac{1}{3}$; $\frac{1}{4}$; $\frac{3}{4}$. Likewise, in the *second* example (Art. 38), $\frac{2}{3}$ is the product $\frac{4}{5} \times \frac{5}{6}$; and $\frac{4}{5}$ may represent the ratio of 60° to 75°, while $\frac{5}{6}$ may represent that of 75° to 90°; of 30° to 36°, etc. Thence arises the triangle of 15°, 75°, 90°, giving the ratios $\frac{1}{5}$, $\frac{1}{6}$, $\frac{5}{6}$. Lastly, in the *third* example (Art. 39), $\frac{4}{5} = \frac{8 \times 9}{9 \times 10}$ where $\frac{8}{9}$ may represent the ratio 72° : 81° and $\frac{9}{10}$ the ratio 81° : 90°.

41. This gives all the usual ratios in musical harmony, excepting $\frac{8}{15}$ and $\frac{15}{16}$. Now, observing that the numerator of the first of these ratios is based on the number 2, while its denominator is based on 3 and 5, we have $\frac{8}{15} = \frac{2}{3} \times \frac{4}{5}$, the product of the two highest ratios afforded by the second and third examples. This affords a triangle of 42°, 48°, 90°.

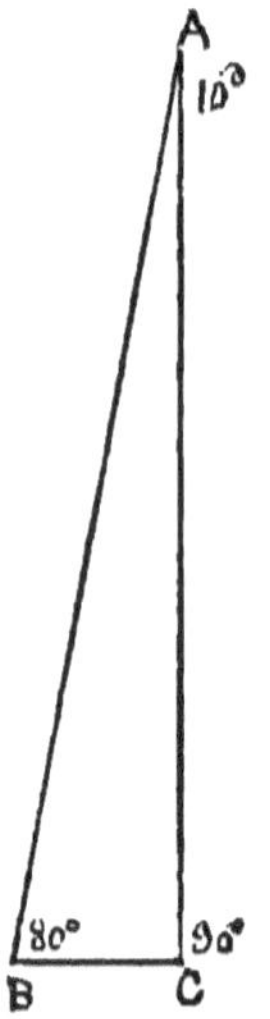

Fig. 7.

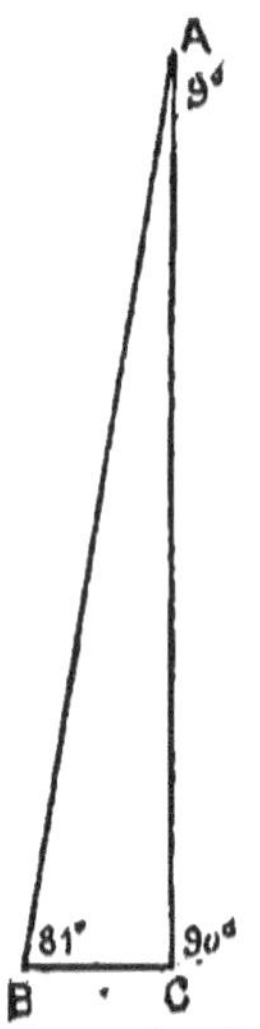

Fig. 8.

See now, also, Figs. 7 and 8, showing the right-angled half of acute isosceles triangles of 20° and 80°, and of 18° and 81°. These halves are right angled triangles of 10°, 80, 90°, and of 9°, 81°, 90°. The first gives ratios 10 : 80, of $\frac{1}{8}$ and 80 : 90, of $\frac{8}{9}$

and the second, ratios, 9 : 81, of $\frac{1}{9}$ and 81 : 90, of $\frac{9}{10}$. Now $\frac{8}{9} = \frac{80}{81}$ of $\frac{9}{10}$ and $\frac{9}{10} = \frac{15}{16} \times \frac{24}{25}$. Here then we have the ratios $\frac{15}{16}$, $\frac{24}{25}$, $\frac{80}{81}$, characteristic of the musical intervals respectively of a diatonic semi-tone, a chromatic semi-tone, and a comma. (Arts. 29, 30, 31.)

Rectangles.

42. The next simplest figure to the triangle, and the most frequent one in architectural and other designs, is the rectangle. A rectangle is resolved by its diagonal into two equal right angled triangles. Hence a rectangle is of harmonious proportions, when the ratios of the angles of one of its component triangles to each other are simple, like those already noticed.

Rectangles enter more largely than any other figure into the design, of a great variety of objects; buildings of all kinds, and their subdivisions, garden compartments; regular furniture; geometrical decorations; railroad cars, books and writing paper; ornamental boxes, carved chests, etc.

With this suggestion, and from the foregoing sufficient statement of principles, the learner can exercise himself in designing many common rectangular things, either by drawing them in the manner shown in Pl. IX., Fig. 2, or by making paper models of them, and this he can do with more pleasure and entertainment, and profit, through the formation of new ideas of his own, than by merely copying any number of given patterns.

EXAMPLE 1. Draw all the rectangles of which Figs. 4 to 8 inclusive are the triangular halves. Also all those indicated in (40, 41) that is, those in which the ratios of the angles of the triangular halves are $\frac{1}{2}$, $\frac{1}{4}$, $\frac{3}{4}$ and $\frac{1}{5}$, $\frac{2}{5}$, $\frac{3}{5}$; etc.

43. *Independent or detached rectangles*, as doors, windows, panels, etc., can be designed in unfettered conformity to the foregoing elementary principles; but rectangles forming the floor, sides and ends of a room are mutually dependent, and cannot always be strictly conformed to these principles. But the discords of form thus arising can be disposed of in two ways, at least.

First. Wainscotings, platforms, cornices, or ornamental bands, may be so adjusted in position and width as to break up an undivided rectangle into subordinate ones of perfect form.

This is somewhat analogous to the fact that in music the chord of the second, which, taken alone, is inharmonious, nevertheless greatly enriches certain combinations of notes into which it enters.

Second. By analogy with temperament (Arts. 32–34), which is mechanically unavoidable in keyed instruments, a noticeable departure from perfect form in some one of a combination of rectangles may be distributed among all of them, thus making it less conspicuous.

44. *Illustration.*—Suppose the principal room in a handsome dwelling to be 36 feet long. Let its floor be divided by its diagonal into triangles of 30°, 60°, 90°. This will give the room a width of 20 ft., 7.7 ins., very nearly.*

Next, taking the longest diagonal of the body of the room as its principal line, let this make an angle of 18° with the floor. This, the diagonal of the floor being about 41 ft., 3.4 ins., will give a height of 13 ft., 10 ins., very nearly, which is sufficient for an apartment of imposing proportions. This height makes with the width, a rectangle for the end of the room, whose diagonal divides it into triangles of about 33°:30'; 56°:30'; 90°, which does not differ seriously from the very simply harmonious one of 36°, 54°, 90°; or from one of 30°, 60°, 90°.

Again, the same height, combined with the length, 36 ft., gives rectangular sides composed of triangles of 21°, 69°, 90°, which thus do not differ greatly from 22°:30'; 67°:30', 90°; or from 18°, 72°, 90°.

45. It now appears that either a slight increase or decrease of the height—neglecting the intangible angle made by the longest, or space diagonal with the floor—would make both the side and end rectangles nearly perfect.

Thus, if the side rectangle contains triangles of 22°:30'; 67°:30'; 90°, the end rectangle would, at the same time, be composed of triangles more nearly than now of 36°:54°:90°, and the height, thereby increased to about 14 ft. 9 ins., would add grandeur to the room.

Otherwise, if the side rectangle were reduced to triangles of 18°, 72°, 90°, the end rectangle would be, more nearly than now,

---

* As found by careful plotting, on a large scale.

APPLICATION TO TRIANGLES AND RECTANGLES. 95

composed of those of 30°; 60°; 90°, where, as in the previous adjustment, the ratios are simple and harmonious. The height, now reduced to about 11 ft. 8 ins., while rather low, yet helps to realize certain ideas of snug home shelter and winter comfort, which are as agreeable in their way, in a cold climate, as the stateliness of a lofty room.

46. To afford a complete view of harmony of form in combined rectangles, it is not enough to secure a harmonious form for each rectangle independently. The like angles of the different rectangles should harmonize by having simple ratios to each other. Thus, in Fig. 9, let ABCH be a floor, with its

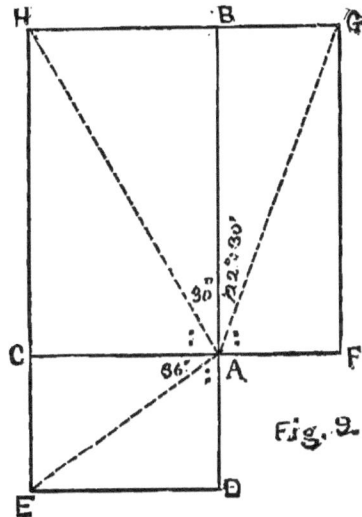

Fig. 9.

diagonal, AH, making an angle of 30° with its edge AB, and ABGF the side wall folded down into the level of the floor, and with a diagonal making an angle of 22°:30' with its base AB. Also, let ADEC be the end wall, similarly folded, and whose diagonal AF will make an angle of not far from 36° with its base. We shall then have the ratios $\frac{22°:30'}{30} = \frac{45}{60} = \frac{3}{4}$; $\frac{22°:30'}{36}$ $= \frac{45}{72} = \frac{5}{8}$; and $\frac{30}{36} = \frac{5}{6}$, all of which are harmonious by their simplicity and relation to the radical harmonic numbers 2, 3, 5.

Ex. 2. Note the ratios between the other three angles indicated in the figure by dots.

Ex. 3. Determine likewise the ratios when the angles of 22°: 30' and 36° are made 18° and 30° respectively.

Ex. 4. Construct a box, or a pasteboard model having the proportions of either of the rooms just described.

CHAPTER V.

GEOMETRIC BEAUTY OF POLYGONS.   GEOMETRICAL DESIGN.

47. *First.* We have seen (Arts. 37–38) that the primary figures representing harmony of form are 1*st,* the *right angled ;* 2*d,* the *equal angled,* and 3*d,* the 36° and 72° *acute angled* isosceles triangles. Then the corresponding *primary rectangles* are those made by placing the halves of these triangles together by their hypothenuses. These rectangles will be the *square ;* the rectangle whose diagonal makes angles of 30° and 60° with its sides ; and the rectangle whose diagonal makes angles of 18° and 72° with its sides.

Second. We have found (Arts. 40, 41) that from these primary triangles others are derived, and from these, in turn, a corresponding series of rectangles proceed.

48. It is interesting next to note that most of the regular polygons, yield simple harmonic ratios, by means of their subdivision into equal triangles, by radii from their centres to their corners.

49. Thus the equilateral triangle, Fig. 10, divides into three

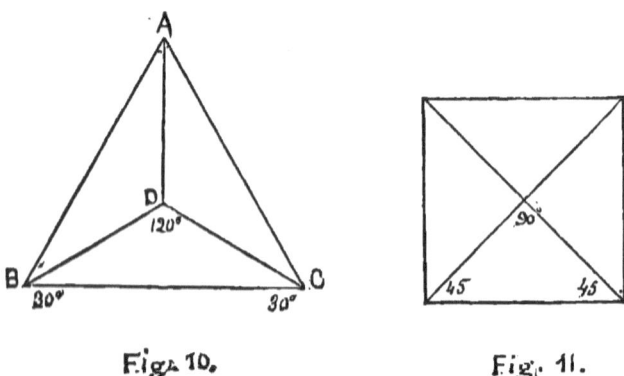

Fig. 10.   Fig. 11.

triangles of 60° and 120°, giving the ratios ¼ and ¼. The square, Fig. 11, divides into triangles of 45° and 90°, giving the ratios ¼ and ½. The regular pentagon, Fig. 12, is composed of triangles of 54° and 72°, giving the ratio ¾.

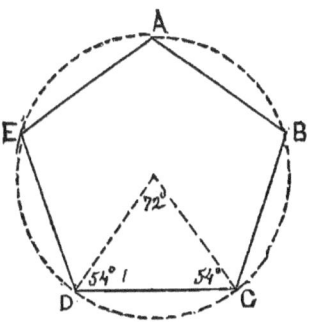

Fig. 12.

Ex. 5. In like manner note the angles and ratios afforded by the other regular polygons, up to the dodecagon or polygon of twelve sides.

50. Proceeding with polygons, as before with rectangles, the only *equal* and *regular* polygons which can combine without leaving unfilled spaces between them, are the equilateral triangle, square and hexagon. Indeed, as the hexagon is itself composed of six equal equilateral triangles, we might say that the equilateral triangle and the square are the only independent figures that can so combine. Only, the equilateral triangle can combine in other ways than in hexagonal groups, so that, practically we may admit the three figures as separate.

51. While combined rectangles constitute the more essential or useful members of many objects, combinations of various regular polygons, or other polygonal pieces founded upon them, may be made, as in Pl. XI.

Ex. 6. Pl. XI., Fig. 1, a five pointed star.
Ex. 7. Pl. XI., Fig. 2, a clover-leaf pattern. where the centres of the circular compartments are the vertices, *a*, *b*, *c*, of the equilateral triangle *abc*.
Ex. 8. Pl. XI., Fig. 3, an equally four armed cross.
Ex. 9. Pl. XI., Fig. 4, an eight pointed star.

52. An immense number of decorative designs, wholly or mostly geometrical, can be based upon the *square*, divided as in

Pl. XI., Fig. 3, into *nine* equal squares, or, as in Fig. 5, into *sixteen;* the latter division being founded on the number 2, the former on the number 3.

52. In many current systems, the lines composing these designs would be located by considerations of *distance*, in some obvious systematic manner. But according to the principles of *direction*, and of *simple ratios between angles*, as properly governing geometrical design, these lines should have *simple angular relations* to each other. Thus, wishing, in Pl. XI., Fig. 3, to place a four-pointed star behind the cross, lines may be drawn from each corner of the large square, as at A, where the lines run to B and C, corners of the furthest arms of the cross. Or they may be drawn, as at D, to corners, E and F of the central small square, or again, so as to divide the *distance* C E or C H, in any given manner. These methods may seem sufficient, because, after a fashion, they are definite and systematic, though the angles at A and D have no simple ratios to each other or to an angle of 90°.

53. But it happens that definiteness and system can be had in another, and, according to the principles before established, a better way. Thus, the lines at d make angles of 30° with each other, giving, with the right angle at d, the ratio $\frac{1}{3}$. Again, the star lines at a include an angle of 45°, thus forming with 90° the ratio $\frac{1}{2}$, while the external angles at a and c are of 22° : 30′ and 67° : 30′ respectively, giving the ratios with 45° of $\frac{1}{2}$ and $\frac{3}{2}$, and with each other of $\frac{1}{3}$. The point at a is less clumsy than that at A; that at d is more decidedly acute than that at D, if decision as to the acuteness be wanted; or, if something nearly like the point D be desired, *with* harmonic angular ratios, it can be had by substituting 36° for the angle of 30° at d. This will give angles of 27° each side of it at d, and thus the ratios $\frac{27}{36} = \frac{3}{4}$; $\frac{27}{90} = \frac{3}{10}$; $\frac{36}{90} = \frac{2}{5}$.

Here it is especially interesting to note, that if the star-point at A be considered well proportioned for a stout one, it is not so, on account of its principle of construction, but because, as shown by calculation, its angle is very nearly one of 54°, which bears the simple ratio, $\frac{3}{5}$ to 90°. Likewise if D be preferred to d, the secret of its superiority lies not in the manner of drawing its sides, but in the fact that its angle is very nearly one of 36°, which would bear to 90° the simple ratio, $\frac{2}{5}$; and would divide the right angle at D into the *varied* parts, 27°, 36°, 27°, instead of the three uniform ones, of 30° as at *d*.

54. Again, Pl. XI., Fig. 5, may serve as a guide to many designs based on a sixteen-fold division of the primitive enclosing square, and made on the principle of simple ratios among the angles. The angles of the corner points are 36°, giving adjacent and alternate angles of 27°, and thence a ratio of $\frac{3}{4}$, and the ratio of 36 to 90 or $\frac{2}{5}$. The outer angles of the intermediate points are 60°, and their inner ones 90°, affording the ratio $\frac{2}{3}$. The obtuse lateral angles of the same points are 105° each, thus introducing, and with evident good effect, ratios of $\frac{60}{105}$ and $\frac{90}{105}$ or $\frac{4}{7}$ and $\frac{6}{7}$ in which the hitherto excluded number, 7, appears. (See Note on Art. 20.)

The angles of 120° and 153°, adjacent to each other, give the ratio $\frac{40}{51}$, so near $\frac{40}{50} = \frac{4}{5}$ that it may be called a tempered $\frac{4}{5}$, while the three angles of 105, 120, 135 give the ratios $\frac{7}{8}$, $\frac{7}{9}$, and $\frac{8}{9}$.

Assembling now the ratios found, in progression, we have—

$$\tfrac{1}{2}-\tfrac{2}{3}-\tfrac{3}{4}-\tfrac{4}{5}-\tfrac{4}{7}-\tfrac{7}{9}$$
$$-\tfrac{6}{7}-\tfrac{7}{8}-\tfrac{8}{9},$$

in which we miss only $\frac{5}{6}$ from the continuous series, while we have in its place $\frac{4}{7}$, bearing to $\frac{4}{5}$ the previous ratio $\frac{2}{3}$; and $\frac{7}{9}$, bearing to $\frac{6}{7}$ the previous ratio $\frac{3}{4}$.

The modification of Pl. XI., Fig. 5, shown in Fig. 13, is pri-

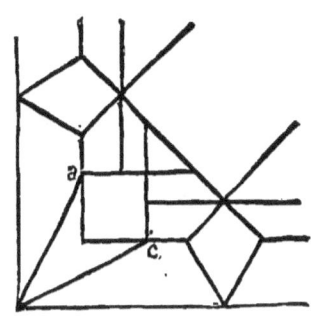

Fig. 13.

marily afforded by enlarging the small corner squares, until they are exactly embraced, as at *a* and *c*, by the sides of the corner points. The arrangement thence suggests other lines, which may or may not be preferred to the less elaborate Fig. 5, on Pl. XI.

Ex. 10–12. Draw Pl. XI., Fig. 3, uniformly; Pl. XI., Fig. 5; and complete Fig. 13 as here begun.

55. Here again, having fully stated and explained the guiding principles, we will, in place of an extended series of copies, all essentially alike in being founded on fanciful relations of *distance*, ask the pupil to exercise himself fully on the following—

Ex. 13. *General Example.*—Prepare several *groups of squares*, with *three slightly separated squares in each group*.

Divide one square of each group into *four* equal squares, another into *nine*, and the other into *sixteen;* in order to secure a regular or symmetrical figure in each case. Then, as in Pl. XI., Fig. 3, place in like compartments of each square some combination of straight lines, located with reference to simple ratios between the *angles* which they make with each other, and between these angles and a right angle.

56. Pl. XI., Fig. 6, shows how pentagons combine, leaving rhombus-formed openings between them. But the angles have simple harmonic relations, and give an agreeable figure. The angles of the pentagons being 108° each, the acute angles of the rhombuses are 36° each, giving the ratio $\frac{1}{3}$, and the obtuse ones are 144°, with which 36° makes the ratio $\frac{1}{4}$, and with which 108° makes the ratio $\frac{3}{4}$.

57. Further geometrical decoration of each pentagon may be made in various ways, which will readily suggest themselves, under the guidance of our uniform principle of simple angular ratios. Thus, by drawing all of the diagonals joining alternate points of a pentagon, a five-pointed star will be formed, Pl. XI., Fig. 1, having a pentagon for its central body, on which stand the points. It is interesting to notice also, that the triangle, ABC, of 36°, 72°, 72°, and described in Art. 39 as representing the *third order* of geometric beauty, founded upon the number 5, is not arbitrarily so described, since it is naturally derived from the regular pentagon, which by its five equal sides and angles, represents in geometry the numeral five in arithmetic.

58. Regular hexagons combine without leaving vacancies be-

tween them, as will be readily seen on trial. They may be easily drawn by means of the equilateral triangles found by dividing the sides of a large equilateral triangle into the same number of equal parts, and drawing parallels to the sides, through the points of division.

Ex. 14. Construct a group of equal regular hexagons.

Octagons, whether regular or with alternate sides smaller than the intermediate ones, combine so as to leave square spaces between them, Pl. XI., Fig. 7. Here the angles of 90° and 135° at any of the corners, give the simple harmonic ratio $\frac{2}{3}$.

The *size* of the corner squares, Fig. 7, will be properly determined by harmonic division of the sides of the original squares from which the octagons are formed. That is, the corners of the small squares should (25, 35) divide the sides of the original squares into parts having simple ratios to each other.

We will here leave rectilinear combinations, having given the guiding principles and illustrations which may enable the learner to make any designs founded upon rectangles and regular polygons, so that they shall possess geometric beauty of form.

59. The principal field for rectangular work will be found in the main divisions of buildings. That of various triangular and polygonal work will consist in subordinate features, bay-windows, summer houses, etc., and in geometrical decorations, such as wood or tile inlaid work, and other geometrical surface decoration.

Ex. 15. Construct Pl. XI., Fig. 6, and inscribe in each pentagon a five-pointed star, as in Fig. 1. Also make the central small pentagons, as *abc*, Fig. 1, black, and the star points lightly shaded.

Ex. 16. Construct Pl. XI., Fig. 7, with any additional geometrical decoration.

Ex. 17. In Ex. 15, make the corner squares smaller, and a square on each side of each. A group of five equal small squares will thus be uniformly placed at each corner of the octagon, and oblong hexagons will be included by the combined squares and octagons.

Ex. 18. Construct Pl. XI., Fig. 8, as it is, then inverted, then turned right for left, and then inverted again; making it two or three times as large as shown. This exercise, often repeated, both on paper and blackboard, will greatly aid in accurately estimating all the most important angles occurring in geometrical decoration, and in various positions.

CHAPTER VI.

CURVILINEAR GEOMETRIC BEAUTY.

Circles and Ellipses.

60. THE principle of *unity*, already defined (Arts. 6–8), together with that of *temperament* (34), will here be remarkably exemplified by considering curves, not separately from the preceding rectilinear figures, but as combined with them.

61. *The circle* is a curve, all of whose points are at a uniform distance, called the *radius*, from a fixed point within it, called its *centre*.

The ellipse is a curve, such that the sum of the distances of each of its points from two fixed points within it is uniform, and equal to the longest line which can be drawn in the curve. These fixed points are called the *foci* of the curve.

According to this definition, the curve, Fig. 14, may be described by a point P, moving so that the sum of its distances

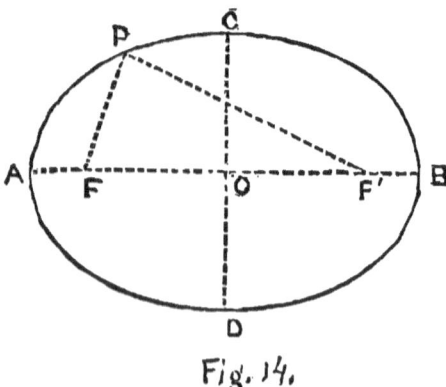

Fig. 14.

from two foci, F and F', is always the same, and equal to the longest chord, or *transverse axis*, AB, of the curve. Many differently shaped ellipses, wide or narrow, may thus be formed according to the distance apart of F and F', while AB remains of fixed length. Pins being fixed at F and F', and a firm thread of the length PFF'P being placed around them, and a pencil point at P, this point, moved so as to keep the string stretched, will trace the ellipse. CD, perpendicular to AB at its middle point, O, is the shorter, minor, or conjugate axis.

62. *Harmonic relations of the triangle, square, and circle.*—Fig. 15, represents a square, 2, 6, 10, 14, each of whose sides

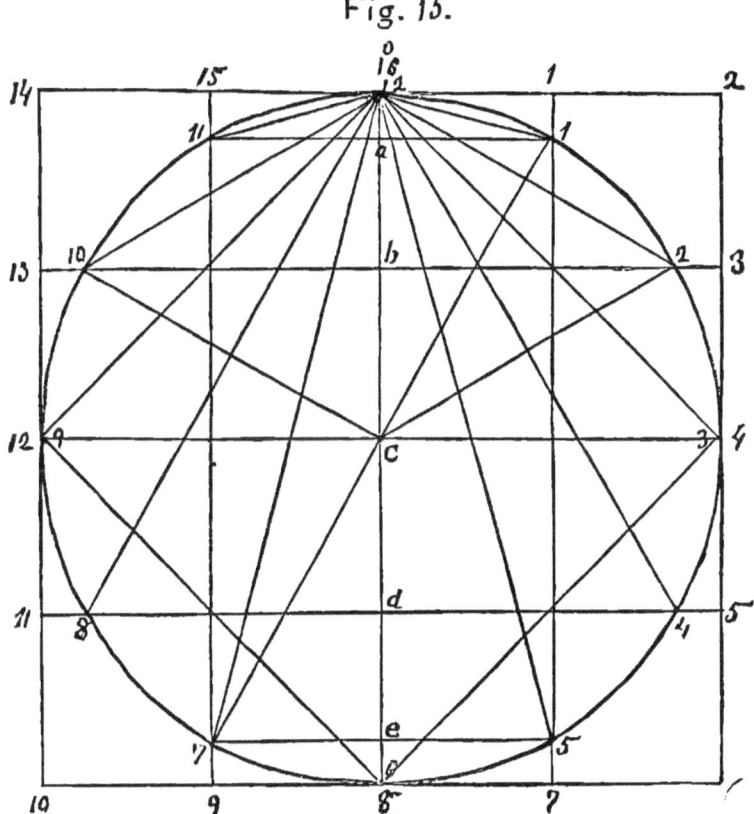

Fig. 15.

is divided into four equal parts. Lines parallel to adjacent sides of the square, through these points of division, divide the area of the square into sixteen equal square parts, as the perimeter is already divided into sixteen linear parts.

If, now, a circle be inscribed in this square, the lines just described will divide its circumference into twelve equal parts, as numbered in the figure, and radii from the points of division will divide the area of the circle into twelve equal parts. Here we have the ratio $\frac{3}{4}$ between both the linear and area divisions.

The inscribed figures are also remarkable.

Remembering that an angle at the circumference of a circle is measured by half the arc of that circumference between its sides:

1°. The inscribed triangle, 3, 9, 0, and therefore, also, its half, 9, c, 0, is one of 45°, 45°, 90°, that is, one of the *first order* (37).

2°. The triangle 8, 4, 0 is an equilateral triangle, whose half, 8, d, 0, is therefore one of 30°, 60°, 90°, that is, one of the *second order* (38).

3°. The triangle 10, 2, 0 is one of 30°, 30°, 120°, whose half, 10, b, 0, is therefore again one of 30°, 60°, 90°.

The foregoing are the most remarkable, in connection with the subsequent figures, though it is interesting to note the following, also.

4°. The triangle 11, 1, 0 is one of 15°, 15°, 150°, whose half, 11, a, 0, is one of 15°, 75°, 90°, giving the ratios $\frac{1}{2}$, $\frac{1}{6}$, $\frac{5}{6}$ (40).

5°. The triangle 7, 5, 0 is one of 30°, 75°, 75°, whose half, 7 e 0, therefore gives again, but as in (2°) with the longest base vertical, a triangle of 15°, 75°, 90°, whose ratios are $\frac{1}{2}$, $\frac{1}{6}$, $\frac{5}{6}$, as before.

Finally, drawing the chords 1, 11 and 5, 7, we have the rectangle 1, 5, 7, 11, belonging to the second order of symmetry (38) in that its half, the triangle 1, 5, 7, is one of 30°, 60°, 90°.

63. *Harmonic relations of ellipses.* The ellipse, being so to speak a somewhat monotonous curve, owing to its double symmetry (Part I., Ch. VII.) which makes its four quarters alike, it is less valuable for many decorative purposes than the egg-formed curves, which will be described further on.

We shall therefore here treat this curve and its relations, less fully than Hay has done, but more completely, so far as the treatment goes; and with much more elementary demonstrations of the properties noted.

In Fig. 16, the rectangle 2', 6', 10', 14', is of the same *proportions* as the inscribed one, 1, 5, 7, 11, in Fig. 15, but larger, its longer side being equal to a side of the circumscribing square in Fig. 15, while its half 2', 6', 10', is a triangle of 30°, 60°, 90°.

By the definition of the ellipse (Art. 61), describe arcs with 4′ and 12′ (on the rectangle) as centres, and the half side, 4′, 2′, as a radius, and they will meet on the line 0′ c′ 8′ at the foci, F and F′. Having the foci, and axes, 0′, 6′, and 3′, 9′, the curve may be drawn by Art. (61), or otherwise, as most convenient.

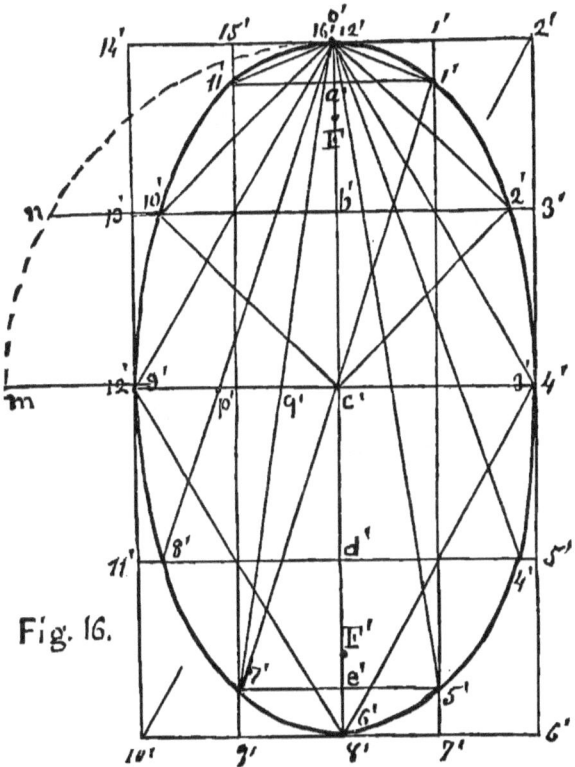

Fig. 16.

So much being done, divide the sides of the rectangle, each into four equal parts, and join the points of division as in the square, which, as before, will divide the rectangle into sixteen equal parts, and the circumference of the ellipse into twelve parts, which, however, are not equal.

64. *We shall now find, by applying a protractor,* the following remarkable results;* naming the inscribed triangles in the same order as for the square.

1°. The right angled triangle 9, c 0 of 45°, 45°, 90°, is

---

* A graduated semi-circle for measuring angles in degrees.

5*

transformed into the semi-equilateral triangle, $9'\,c'\,0'$, of $30°$, $60°, 90°$, that is, from one of the *first*, to one of the *second* order of symmetry.

2°. The triangle $8\,d\,0$, of $30°$, $60°$, $90°$, is transformed into the triangle $8'\,d'\,0'$ which is sensibly one of $18°$, $72°$, $90°$, that is, from one of the *second* to one of the *third* order of symmetry.

3. The triangle $10\,b\,0$ is transformed into $10'\,b'\,0'$ of $45°, 45°$, $90°$, that is from the *second*, to the *first* order of symmetry.

4°. Taking the supplementary triangles; $11\,a\,0$ is replaced by $11'\,a'\,0'$ which is almost exactly one of $18°$, $72°$, $90°$.

5°. Also, $7\,e\,0$ is transformed into $7'\,e'\,0'$, a triangle sensibly of $9°, 81°, 90°$, giving the ratios $\frac{1}{6}$, $\frac{1}{15}$, $\frac{9}{10}$.

65. Demonstrations.* We shall uniformly call the radius of the circle, Fig. 15 (equal to $c'\,0'$, Fig. 16) $= 1$. Then—

1°. *The triangle* $9'\,c'\,0'$. The rectangle, Fig. 16, is, by construction, one whose triangular half, $2', 6', 10'$, is a triangle of $30°, 60°, 90°$. The triangular quarter, $9'\,c'\,0'$, of the rectangle, is evidently of like proportions, and hence is *exactly* a triangle of $30°, 60°, 90°$.

To find the value of $c'\,9'$, refer to the triangle $c\,e\,7$, Fig. 15, also evidently similar to the preceding, and we have

$$ce : e7 :: c'0' : c'9'$$

that is, $\frac{1}{2}\sqrt{3} : \frac{1}{2} :: 1 : c'9'$.

Hence $c'9' = \dfrac{\frac{1}{2}}{\frac{1}{2}\sqrt{3}} = \dfrac{1}{\sqrt{3}}$

2°. *The triangle* $10'\,b'\,0'$. Here it is necessary to explain, first, that a perpendicular as $b\,10$, or $b'\,10'$, from a point of the circumference to a diameter or axis, of a circle, or ellipse, is called an *ordinate* to that diameter. Also, if the circle, Fig. 15, be revolved about the diameter $0, 6$, until the diameter $3\,c\,9$ be inclined to the paper so as to appear of the length $3'\,c'\,9$, the ordinate $b'\,10'$ will be parallel in space to $c'\,9'$, both being equally inclined to the paper at b' and c'. Perpendiculars,

---

*These, given by Hay in an appendix, and by the methods of analytical geometry, suited therefore only to advanced students, are here given arithmetically in a way suited to pupils acquainted with the elements of geometry.

from 10′ and 9′ in space, to the paper, will be parallel, and we shall thus have the two similar triangles standing on $b'\,10'$ and $c'\,9'$, which when placed together, so that $b'\,10'$ falls on $c'\,9'$, and then turned down into the paper will appear as in Fig. 17.

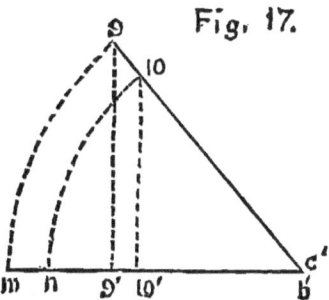
Fig. 17.

Then we evidently have $b'\,10' : b'\,10 :: c'\,9' : c'\,9$. That is, see Figs. 15, 16, the ordinate $b'\,10'$ of an ellipse, *is to* the corresponding ordinate, $b\,10$, of the circle described on the longer axis of the ellipse as a diameter, *as* the semi-conjugate axis, $c'\,9'$, of the ellipse, *is to* its semi-transverse axis, $c\,9$ ($=c'\,0'$, Fig. 16).

But $b\,10 = \tfrac{1}{2}\sqrt{3}$ and $c'\,9' = \dfrac{1}{\sqrt{3}}$, hence, only changing the order of the proportion,

$$c\,9 : c'\,9' :: b\,10 : b'\,10';$$

that is $\qquad 1 : \dfrac{1}{\sqrt{3}} :: \tfrac{1}{2}\sqrt{3} : b'\,10.$

Therefore $\qquad b'\,10 = \dfrac{\tfrac{1}{2}\sqrt{3}}{\sqrt{3}} = \tfrac{1}{2} = b'\,0'.$

Hence the triangle $10'\,b'\,0'$ is exactly one of 45°, 45°, 90°.

3°. *The triangle* $8'\,d'\,0'$. Here $d'\,0' = \tfrac{3}{2}$ and $8'\,d' = \tfrac{1}{2}$. Then to find the distance $c'p'$ corresponding to $8'\,d'$, when $d'\,0'$ is reduced to $c'\,0'$ or 1, we have

$$\tfrac{3}{2} : 1 :: \tfrac{1}{2} : c'p',$$

whence $\qquad c'p' = \dfrac{\tfrac{1}{2}}{\tfrac{3}{2}} = \tfrac{1}{3}.$

Now from a table of natural tangents* (see works on trigonometry or surveying), we find that $\tfrac{1}{3}$ is the natural tangent of $18° : 26' :$, or more exactly, of $18° : 26' : 6''$.

The triangle $8'\,d'\,0'$ is thus almost exactly one of $18°, 72°, 90°$, the slight difference being an illustration of temperament, (Art. 34), in this case the modification of the perfect triangle by the constraining effect of combining it with an ellipse, under a rigid system, that of the sixteen-fold equal division of the circumscribing rectangle.

4°. *The triangle* $7'\,e'\,0'$. Here $c'e' = ce$, Fig. 15, (65, 2.°)

But $ce = \sqrt{(c\,7)^2 - (e\,7)^2} = \sqrt{1-\tfrac{1}{4}} = \sqrt{\tfrac{3}{4}} = \tfrac{1}{2}\sqrt{3}$

Then $0'e' = 1 + \tfrac{1}{2}\sqrt{3}$ and $e'\,7' = \tfrac{1}{2}c'\,9' = \dfrac{1}{2\sqrt{3}}$.

To find $c'q'$, or $e'\,7'$ reduced to correspond with $0'c'$, or 1, we have,

$$0'e' : 0'c' :: e'\,7' : c'q'$$

or
$$1 + \tfrac{1}{2}\sqrt{3} : 1 :: \dfrac{1}{2\sqrt{3}} : c'q'$$

whence $c'q' = \dfrac{\tfrac{1}{2\sqrt{3}}}{1 + \tfrac{1}{2}\sqrt{3}} = \dfrac{\tfrac{1}{\sqrt{3}}}{2 + \sqrt{3}} = \dfrac{1}{2\sqrt{3} + 3} = 0.1547$

which is the natural tangent of $8° : 48'-$, showing that $7'e'\,0'$ is very nearly a triangle of $9°, 81°, 90°$.

---

* If the hypotenuse, O B, Fig. 18, of a right-angled triangle be taken as a radius, as shown by the arc Bb, and called 1, the other sides will be called, AB, the natural *sine*, and OA the natural *cosine* of the angle O, at the centre.

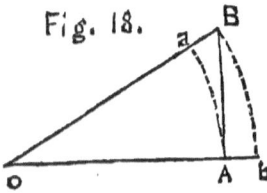

Fig. 18.

But if the side, OA, of the right angle, be taken as such radius, as indicated by the arc Aa, the *other* side, AB, will be the natural *tangent* of the same angle.

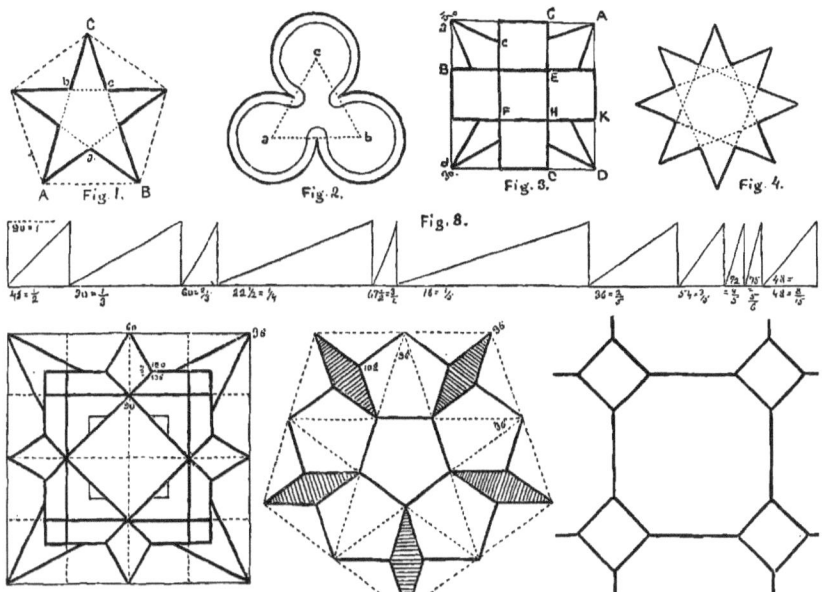

5°. *The triangle* 11' a' 0'. Here 0' a' = $1 - \frac{1}{2}\sqrt{3}$ and a' 11' = $\frac{1}{2\sqrt{3}}$. Then to find the angle at 0' to a radius of 1, we must proceed as in 4°, whence $1 - \frac{1}{2}\sqrt{3} : 1 :: \frac{1}{2\sqrt{3}}$: tang. a' 0' 11'.

That is, tang. a' 0' 11' = $\frac{\frac{1}{2\sqrt{3}}}{1-\frac{1}{2}\sqrt{3}} = \frac{\frac{1}{\sqrt{3}}}{2-\sqrt{3}} = \frac{1}{2\sqrt{3}-3}$

= 2.15425 = the natural tangent of 65° : 6' +. Hence the triangle 0' a' 11' is not a very close approximation to one of 22° : 30', 67° : 30', 90°.

66. Proceeding in like manner, beginning with a rectangle composed of two triangles of the third order of symmetry 18°, 72°, 90° (Art. 39), we should find like curious and interesting results. Thus 0', 2', 10', Fig. 16, will then become an equilateral triangle, or its half, one of 30°, 60°, 90°; 0', 3', c' will become a triangle of 18°, 72°, 90°, and 0' 4' d', one of 10°, 80°, 90°, etc. And, in general, the triangle on 2', 10' of a series of ellipses thus formed, will be of the same form as the one on 3' c' 9' of the next preceding ellipse, and so on; the one on 4' 8' being of the next higher degree in the series of triangles, and the one whose half determines the form of the circumscribing rectangle of the next ellipse.

Elliptical Designs.

These may be formed by combining ellipses, as indicated in the following examples, and in other ways which the pupil may invent. (See Part I., p. 40.)

Ex. 19. Construct the next three ellipses to Fig. 16, indicated in the last article.

Ex. 20. Combine the circle and the different ellipses, by pairs, replacing the left hand half of Fig. 15, by the left hand half of Fig. 16, for example.

Ex. 21. Proceed in like manner with either Figs. 15 or 16, and either of the ellipses of Ex. 19.

Ex. 22. Making Fig. 16 larger, so that 3', 9' shall be equal to 3, 9 in Fig. 15, replace the lower half of Fig. 15 by that of the new Fig. 16. Do the like with the ellipses of Ex. 19.

CHAPTER VII.

CURVILINEAR GEOMETRIC BEAUTY. OVALS.

Natural and Artificial Curves.

67. *A natural curve* is formed so that every point of it is located by one and the same law of construction; as when a circle is drawn with a pair of dividers carrying a pencil, whose describing point moves in obedience to the one law of always being at a *uniform distance from a fixed point*.

68. A curve is also natural, when it arises by cutting the surface of some simple body—also formed according to some one law—by a plane or by some other simple surface. Thus, a cone is formed by revolving a right-angled triangle about either of the sides of the right angle; and the curves which arise by cutting its curved surface by any plane are natural curves.

69. *An artificial curve*, on the contrary, is built up of separate arcs, of circles of different radii, or of some other kind of curve, placed tangent to each other.

70. Thus the natural ellipse, Fig. 14, is described, according to Art. (61) by a continuous movement of one kind.

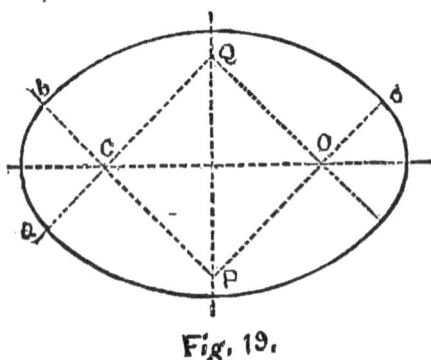

Fig. 19.

71. The artificial ellipse may be composed in various ways of four or more circular arcs, one way being shown in Fig. 19,

where C, O, P, Q, are the centres of the two pairs of arcs, as *ab*, and *bc*, there used. But the resulting figures are all more or less unsightly curves, in that they appear swelled at the middle of each arc, and flattened at the junctions of the different arcs, owing to the sudden and great changes of radius which occur at the latter points.

The Egg-Form, or Oval.

72. *This curve invites examination* by its constant occurence in Nature, and its great beauty. But in turning from Nature to Geometry, we find no mention made of egg-formed curves in ordinary treatises, while in the more extended works on the higher curves, we find them occasionally as detached portions of curves having a complex law of construction, and which consist of two or more separate branches.

73. This absence of egg-curves, constructed by any simple rule, may account for the customary substitution, in practical drawing books, of artificial egg-curves, composed of circular

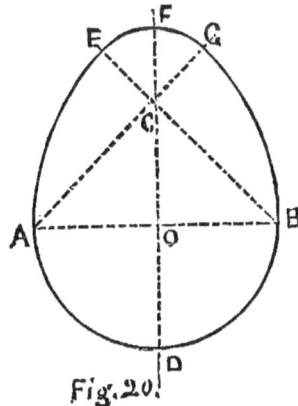

Fig. 20.

arcs, as in Fig. 20, where A D B is a semi-circle; A E and B G are arcs described from B and A, respectively as centres, C the intersection of their radii, being the centre of the arc E F G.

74. *Hay's composite ellipse.*—Still, it is desirable, both for the sake of conformity to Nature, and of completing a system of geometric beauty, that an oval curve should be found, as naturally and intimately associated with the various harmonic

triangles (37–39) as the circle is with the square, or the ellipse with the rectangle.

Hay perceived and stated this want, and, in his search to supply it, devised the egg-curve which he called the *composite ellipse*, Fig. 21. Here, the points A, B, C, are foci, and D is the describing point. That is, pins being set at A, B, C, D and an inelastic string tied tightly around the four, the pin at D is then replaced by a moving pencil point, as at P, Fig. 14, and this pencil, moved so as to keep the string tense, will describe the egg-curve shown in Fig. 21. Comparing this with Fig. 20, the curve will evidently consist of several elliptical

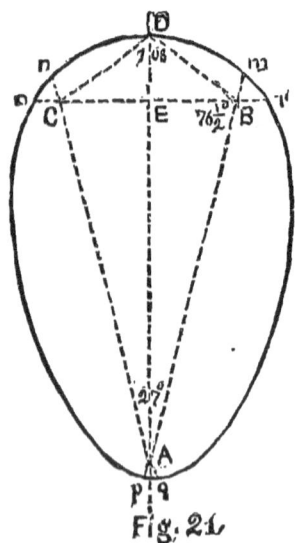

Fig. 21.

arcs; first mDn, with B and C for its foci; second no, with A and B for foci; third, op, with A and C for foci; next, the short arc pq with B and C again as foci, etc. The curves thus formed are divided by Hay into five "classes," according as the angle at D is 90°, 108°, 120°, 135°, 144°, these all having simple ratios to 180°. Each class is then divided into as many "degrees" as there may be angles chosen at A having simple ratios to the fixed class angle at D.

Thus a great variety of egg-forms, or ovals, including many oblate ones, are formed; as when, for example, the angles at A and D are made 90° and 135° respectively. All these can readily be traced, by the student who would gratify his curiosity to know how they would appear.

75. *Objections.* All this seems simple and ingenious, but—
First, the guiding idea of simple ratios between the angles of the same right-angled triangle as A E B is partly, at least, abandoned. Thus Fig. 21, $13\frac{1}{2} = \frac{27}{153} = \frac{3}{17}$ a very odd ratio.
$76\frac{1}{2}$

Second. The curve is artificial, and not natural, as much so as are Figs. 19 and 20, in that it is built up of arcs of another kind of curve.

Third, accordingly, pottery, and other designs formed with it, fail to perfectly satisfy the eye of persons of taste, not knowing how these designs were formed. That is, these designs imperfectly realized a good general idea, just to the extent that these curves were artificial, and also perhaps inappropriately combined.

76. *The natural method.* Happily, there remains another path which promises to lead to the desired curve. It is to be remembered that curves never occur in nature as separate independent things, but only as the outlines or sections of the surfaces of bodies. Hence, in place of seeking among collections of all the curves which accident or the wit of man have suggested, we shall seek some surface whose sections will be egg-curves or ovals.

One of the best for our purpose is the following.

77. Let A C B, Fig. 22, represent a semi-circle, standing perpendicularly to the paper, and thus appearing to coincide with its diameter A B, which is supposed to be in the surface of the paper. Then A O B will represent this semi-circle, after revolving it over into the paper, about its fixed diameter A B as an axis. Next, let A O B be an isosceles right-angled triangle, inscribed in this semi-circle, and produce its sides at pleasure. Transform this triangle into any other, as *a* O *b*, in which one vertex shall remain at O, and the altitude shall still coincide with O C, and make the angles at *a* and *b* with any simple ratio to each other. In the figure, this ratio is $\frac{1}{2}$, the angles at *a* and *b* being respectively of 30° and 60°.

So much being done, mark the points *b*, C, *a* on the edge of a slip of paper, and then adjust the position of the slip by trial, which can easily be done, so that the distances $a\,C$ and $b\,C$ shall be included, as shown at $a_1\,c_1$ and $b_1\,c_1$, between the lines O A and O C, and O B and O C, the lines distinguished by stars.

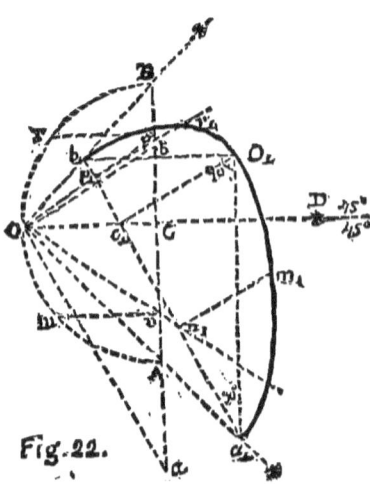

Fig. 22.

Then, assuming any points, as n and p, equidistant from C for convenience, draw $n\,m$ and $p\,r$ perpendicular to A B; and draw O n and O p, and note their intersections, n_1 and p_1 with $a_1\,b_1$. Also note c_1. Finally, at $n_1\,c_1\,p_1$ draw perpendiculars to $a_1\,b_1$, and make $n_1\,m_1 = n\,m$; $c_1\,O_1 = CO$; $p_1\,r_1 = pr$. Then the curve $a_1\,O_1\,b_1$ will be that semi-oval which circumscribes the triangle $a_1\,O_1\,b_1$ of 30°, 60°, 90° derived from the triangle A O B as described, that is, so that O D *bisects* the angle A O B.

78. *Variations* from Fig. 22. These may be made in three ways.*

1°. By dividing the angle A O B equally, or otherwise.

2°. By making the ratio of the angles, a and b, of the transformed triangle $a\,O\,b$, either the same as, or different from that of the two angles into which A O B is divided.

3°. By making the transformed triangle $a\,O\,b$ (or $a\,S\,b$—see Art. 79) right angled, or not, at O.

79. *Illustrations.* Of Figs. 23 to 30, inclusive, each illus-

---

* I find by trial, that, other things being the same, the position of O, as the centre of the radials O a_1, O n, O p, etc., does not affect the form of the oval.

CURVILINEAR GEOMETRIC BEAUTY. OVALS. 115

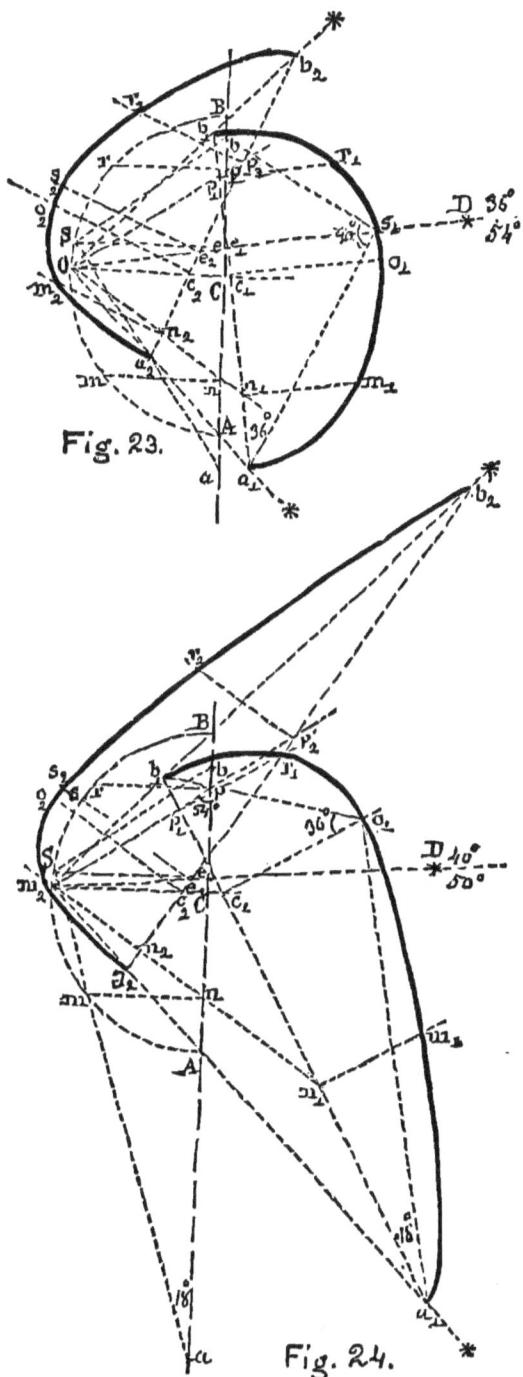

Fig. 23.

Fig. 24.

trates one or more of these variations. Similar points having the same letters on all of them, and the construction of all being the same, with one exception, next mentioned, repeated description is unnecessary.

But note, that when the angle A O B is divided unequally, as in Figs. 23, 24, etc., the vertex of the transformed triangle moves from O to S, the summit of a perpendicular to A B from its intersection, e, with the dividing line O D, which then no longer coincides with O C.

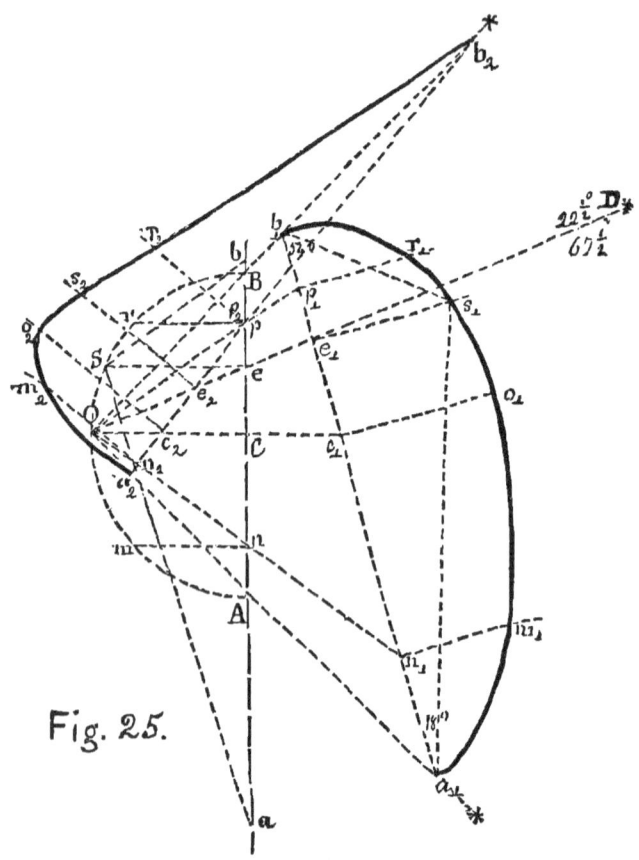

Fig. 25.

Returning to the illustrations; In Fig. 23, a S b is a right angle, while in Fig. 24, it is not. In Fig. 22, A O B is divided equally, and in Figs. 23, 24, etc., it is not; the degrees in each division being marked at D. In Fig. 23, the angles at a and b

have the same ratio as the parts of A O B, while in Fig. 24, they do not.

80. *Pairs of ovals.* Notice, *further*, that whenever A O B is divided unequally by OD, we can obtain *two ovals* from the same transformed triangle $a\,S\,b$; according as either segment as $a\,e$, or $b\,e$, of its base is inscribed in the larger, or smaller of the angles into which A O B is divided, as at $b_1\,e_1 = be$, or $a_2\,e_2 = be$, in Figs. (23—26).

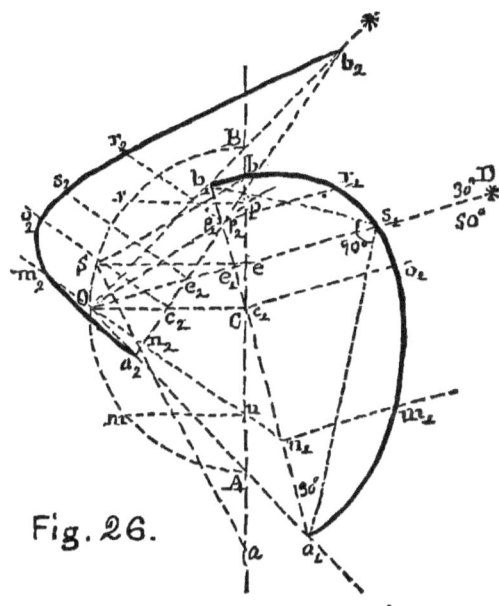

Fig. 26.

81. *Results of the variations.*—1. The more acute the angles at a and b, the longer, and more nearly pointed, the oval becomes.

2°. The greater the difference between the angles at a and b, the greater is the difference in the form of the two ends of the oval.

3°. But when the *shorter* segment be of the base ab is inscribed in the *larger* of the two unequal angles into which AOB may be divided, the more unequal these angles, the more acute is the oval at the end at the acute angle, and obtuse at the opposite end, as is successively more and more strikingly shown by the oval $a_2\,o_2\,b_2$ in Figs. 23, 24, 25.

82. *To make a flat oval*—one broader than it is long—the

118 FREE-HAND GEOMETRICAL DRAWING.

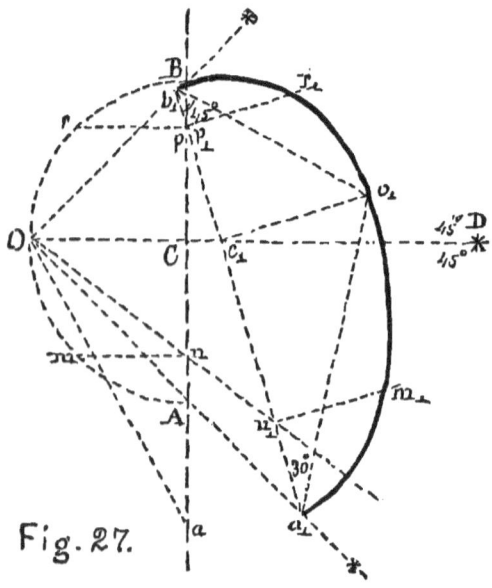

Fig. 27.

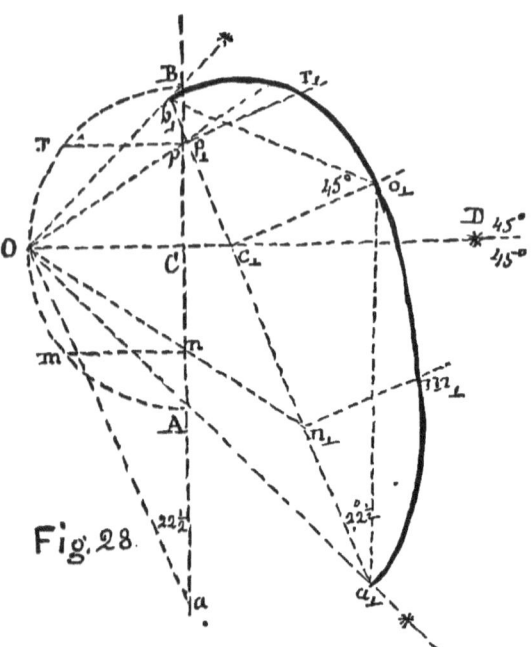

Fig. 28.

base ab, Figs. 29, 30, of the transformed triangle, must be shorter than the greatest width, 2 O C, or 2 S e, of the oval. The axis, $a_1 b_1$, of the oval, being thus brought nearer to O, the

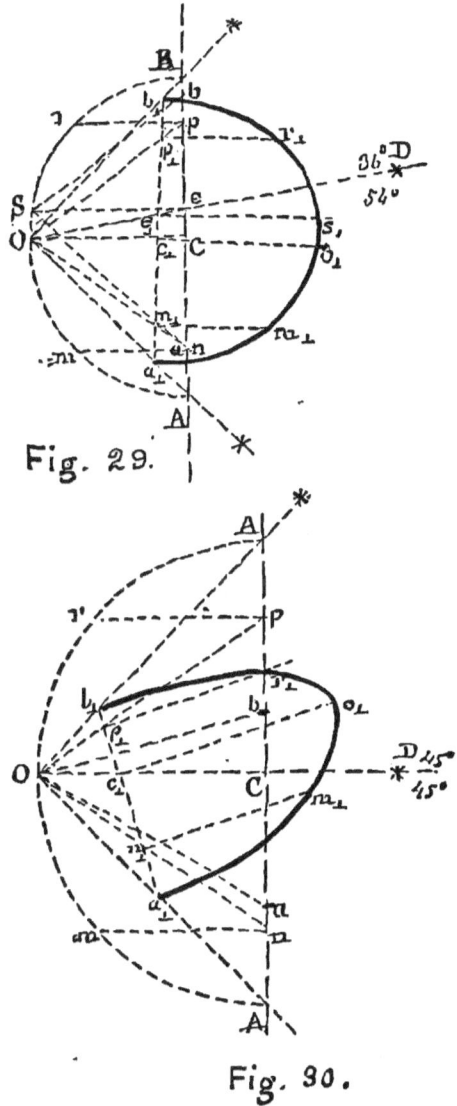

Fig. 29.

Fig. 30.

semi-circle A O B should be larger, to give an oval of the desired size.

83. Only half ovals are shown, in order to avoid confusing

the figures. They will exhibit themselves better by completing them; the two halves on each side of $a_1 b_1$, or $a_2 b_2$, being just alike in all the figures.

With these explanations and illustrations, pupils and practical designers will be put in possession of the means of constructing ovals of every possible variety of form, and based upon definite angular relations.

Any oval can then, if desired, be enlarged or diminished in *size*, without altering its *form*, and without the labor of entirely reconstructing it, by either of the methods explained in PART I., Pl. II., Figs. 7, 8, 9.*

Industrial Applications.

84. *The industrial applications* of the ovals now described, both to objects of utility and beauty, are so numerous that, for want of space, we can only name some of them, in connection with the principles governing their design, and illustrated by a few sketches. But more than this is unnecessary, for as the designer is furnished with the necessary principles to guide him, he is made independent of multiplied copies to be merely imitated without further thought.

Among the most important of such objects, are those of pottery and glass; as pitchers, bowls, vases, goblets, fruit-dishes, gas-shades, etc.; and of metal, as tea-sets, butter dishes, vases, lamps, urns, etc.; also architectural ornaments, mouldings, railings etc.; and church, school, hall and house furniture.

85. *Free application.*—The ear is the best instrument for testing the musical beauty which results from the combination of musical chords, separately agreeable, into a piece of music. Likewise the eye is the best instrument for testing the beauty

---

* The advanced student, if acquainted with Descriptive Geometry, will recognize the surface from which these ovals are cut as a *right conoid*, whose directrices are the semi-circle ACB, and a vertical at O, equal to AC, and whose elements are all parallel to the paper.

Besides the conoid, egg forms can be cut from the "annular torus," a ring of circular or elliptical section, by planes parallel to its axis, and cutting it in two curves.

PL. XII.

of compound forms, made by combining separately pleasing elementary forms.

Moreover, as we have seen, very many ovals can inscribe the same harmonic triangle. Thus, in various ways, it is evident, that, in the higher forms of curvilinear beauty, we depart further and further from the domain of rules alone, and that the principle of freedom (Art. 11) or intuitive perception of beauty prevails; just as in music, a piece may be composed, strictly according to rules, and yet be utterly destitute of beauty, while another may be very beautiful, and yet the secret of its beauty be inexpressible by any rule.

Hence, for all purposes of application of the ovals here described, it is sufficient to direct the designer to construct a large number of them on card-board, classifying them according to the distinctions given in Art. (78), and then to combine them tangentially to each other, or intersecting each other also, as in Pl. XII., until the outline formed by their combination satisfies his eye; or is pronounced beautiful by persons of taste, independently of each other, and, better still, unbiassed by a knowledge of the method by which the design was produced.

And here note, that angles formed by the meeting of curves, are, for purposes of comparison, to be estimated by the tangents to those curves at the point of intersection of the curves.

86. *Application, governed by rules.* The ovals here described are so graceful, that they combine together in graceful forms almost as readily as different plant leaves do in a bouquet. Still, if ornamental forms, like those of Pl. XII., are to be designed in a *strictly systematic manner*, instead of by merely *satisfying the eye by trial*, three points may be kept in mind while making the design.

First; If different ovals are to be used in the same design, those may be chosen in which the angles of each of the inscribed triangles form harmonious, or simple ratios with those of the others.

Second; The angles made by the axes of auxiliary ovals, with the vertical axis of the entire figure, as in the neck and foot of Fig. 1, may have a simple ratio to 90°.

Third; According to Art. (35) the axis of the figure may be divided by the different members of the entire design, into segments having simple ratios to the whole height.

87. The designs on Pl. XII., were mostly formed by the first method (85) that of satisfying the eye by trial. Yet the segments of the heights are, generally, very nearly if not exactly simple ratios of the whole heights. These designs are not offered as models of oval composition, but only to indicate the manner of combining ovals in forming regular objects with curved outlines.

Fig. 1, for example, is composed of the oval $a_1 s_1 b_1$ of Fig. 25, for its body, with a part of $a_2 s_2 b_2$, Fig. 23, for its neck, and of the end at a_1 of $a_1 s_1 b_1$, Fig. 22, for its foot. From this beginning, innumerable minor modifications can be made by the pupil or designer, by taking variously proportioned ovals for the body, and various portions of different ovals for the neck and foot, until the most satisfactory forms shall be attained. In like manner, each of the following examples may be variously modified.

88. Pl. XII., Fig. 2, represents a glass fruit dish, the body composed of the lower portion of Fig. 30, ending a little above its line $c_1 o_1$, of greatest width; and the foot composed of an arc of $a_2 s_2 b_2$, Fig. 24, in the vicinity of s_2. Slight variations in the fashion of the body would make its brim just on the line, $c_1 o_1$, of greatest width, or a little below that line.

The top of the dish, being of *less* diameter than the body below, expresses reserve. When, as in the last modification mentioned, the top diameter is greatest, generous freedom is expressed. Or, leaving sentiment for utility, the first form is better adapted to carry fluid contents without spilling, and the second, to supporting a pyramid of fruit.

89. Pl. XII., Fig. 3, represents a garden vase. The outline of the upper member is an arc of the oval in Fig. 22, from O_1 towards a_1, and is superior in two ways to an outline composed, as is sometimes done, of a straight line tangent to a circular arc. First, it is wholly curved. Second, the curvature constantly varies, instead of being uniform, that is, monotonous, as in a circular arc.

The middle member is composed of the larger segment of a smaller oval of the same form as that of Fig. 29, and is much finer than a simple semi-circle, though the difference is not great on the scale of the figure.

The lower member is composed of various mouldings, all the curved portions of which would, when of full size, be composed of arcs at the tip of some of the more pointed ovals.

90. Pl. XII., Fig. 4, is a two-handled jug, in which, to secure flowing combined outlines, and an absence of straight lines, the form of the actual piece of pottery from which the figure was taken, was modified by giving a very slight curvature to the handles, taking for this purpose the straightest portion of the oval $a_2 s_2 b_2$ of Fig. 24.

Also the decision expressed by an exact right angle is secured by taking the top outline of the oval $a_2 s_2 b_2$ of Fig. 26, for the curve of the top of the figure. A portion of a new oval, not shown in any of the diagrams, forms the body of the jug. It was formed from a circle of a diameter equal to the greatest diameter of the jug, with the angle A O B bisected, and the inscribed triangle of the half oval having base angles, a and b, of 10° and of 60°.

91. Pl. XII., Fig. 5, represents a portable gas-light, in which the outline of the shade consists of a little more than the most flattened half, $o_1 s_1 b_1$, of the small oval similar to Fig. 29, the exact half, ending at the double lines near the top. The standard is formed of an arc of the acute oval used in Fig. 4, but broken, to secure shadow and variety, by the two rings. Strictly, and when of full size, the moulding of these rings should be in ovals.

92. Pl. XII., Fig. 6, represents a fruit dish wholly composed of arcs of the oval, of Fig. 30. The flatter half, enlarged a trifle, is taken for the body of the dish, terminating on the line $c_1 s_1$ of greatest width of the oval. The standard is composed of nearly the whole of the outline of the more convex half, $a_1 o_1$, of the same oval.

The Method by Co-ordinates.

93. Compound, or waving curves may be sketched by a method suggested by that of finding the location of a stream, or other irregular line, in a survey, viz., by distances to the given

line, measured perpendicularly from points at given distance apart on a fixed straight line of reference, as ab in Fig. 31.

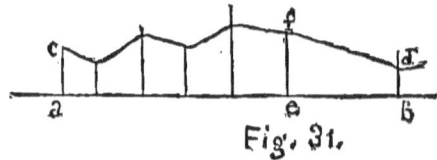

Fig. 31.

But in applying this method to the free design of some ideal line of beauty, we are no longer bound by given distances either on, or from ab, but can, according to the principles of this Part III., substitute angular ratios for them.

Thus, in Fig. 32, the left hand profile, A, is determined by co-ordinate distances. The height 04 is divided by trial into

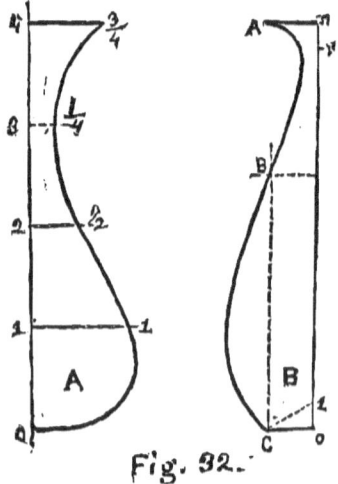

Fig. 32.

four equal parts, then 11 equals one of those parts, the next equals half of 01; the next, one-fourth of 01; and the top width is three-fourths of 01. This seems simple and systematic, but the result is less pleasing than B, or than Fig. 33, which it somewhat resembles. And we venture to say that any design, made like A, Fig. 32, by related distances, will only happen to be pleasing, as a result of repeated trials, while forms like B, and Fig. 33, composed of arcs of ovals, (85, 86) will almost always be graceful.

Fig. 33 is composed of an arc of the side of $a^1 O_1 b_1$, Fig. 22, from A to B, and of the pointed end of $a_1 s_1 b_1$, Fig. 26. It be-

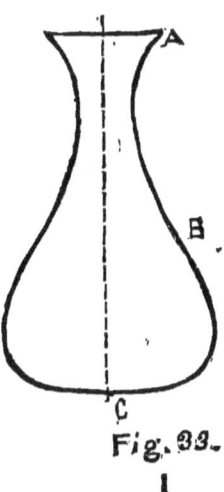

Fig. 33.

longs to that class of vase forms, which have a tapering neck and a somewhat sharply curved body, and is decidedly superior in configuration to like forms composed of arcs of composite ellipses.

Ex. 23. Apply the principles of this chapter to the designing of a cup and saucer.
Ex. 24. Design, likewise, a garden urn or vase.
Ex. 25. Do. A fountain.
Ex. 26. Do. A summer-house, applying the principles of Chapters IV. and V., to the rectilinear parts.
Ex. 27. Do. A library table.
Ex. 28. Do. A parlor stove.
Ex. 29. Do. A flower garden.
Ex. 30. Do. A pulpit.

CHAPTER VIII.

GEOMETRIC SYMBOLISM.

Definitions, and General Illustrations.

94. AMONG the elements of geometric beauty, but of a very different kind from those of harmonious proportion thus far explained, is the symbolism of geometrical figures, or the analogies between some of their properties and certain elements of life.

Examples of such analogies may here form an appropriate conclusion. They are generally expressed by the words, type, emblem, symbol, of which the last only will be particularly considered.

95. A *symbol* is anything apparent to *sense*, which yet, of itself, *naturally* expresses, represents, or suggests to the mind some truth of *life;* the natural counterpart in the world of *matter*, of something corresponding to it in the world of *mind*.

In this natural correspondence, a symbol is quite different from an emblem, or a type, as may be sufficiently seen by reflection on the common use of the words. Thus every one says, "the national *emblem*," speaking of his country's flag, but not the national symbol. Here, the connection between the *thing* and the *thought* is dependent on association, and mutual agreement, and not on inherent natural correspondence and may be equally strong, whatever the thing chosen may be.

A *type* belongs to the same general form of existence as the thing typified. It is a part, taken as a representative of the whole; a specimen, as the representative of a class; a lower form, as a representative of a higher form of being or action of the same kind.

96. *To illustrate:* The mingled verdure and bloom of spring, are *symbols* of the freshness, modesty and promise of unperverted youth. The tints and fruits of autumn, or a sunset in

crimson and golden light, are *symbols* of the close of a worthy, or a splendid career.

A monument is an *emblem* of departed greatness. A *broken* monument is a *symbol* of a broken life. The American flag is an *emblem* of the nation's life. Its rivers are the *symbol* of the *scale of its life*, its ideas, and its actions. Its best, and its worst, treatment of the Indians, are *types* of its highest and of its lowest humanity seen in all other relations of life.

Again: Water, by its properties, is a *type* of fluids generally. The ocean is of itself, because of its apparent boundlessness, a *symbol* of eternity.

The oak, with its mighty and horizontal arms, is a *symbol* of self-sufficient rough and rugged strength, and independence. The elm is a *symbol* of united strength and grace, and thus of culture. Hence, apart from practical convenience, the avenues of cultured towns are appropriately lined with elms, rather than with oaks.

With the *idea* of symbols thus awakened, the following examples of geometric symbols will suffice to lead the mind into action on the subject.

Geometric Illustrations.

97. *A straight line* is the symbol of repose, monotony, permanence and deadness. It is so by reason of its monotony of form, in having but one unchanging direction. It is therefore adapted to situations where repose, in the shape of fixedness or permanence, is natural or desirable.

Thus, in the fervent tropical heats of a land like Egypt, where vigorous activity is to be dreaded, and the repose of utter inaction courted, the main outlines of the buildings, naturally and forcibly express these facts by the free use of straight lines, and *these*, as the boundaries of most massive and heavily proportioned forms. Stout and short vertical columns, mile-long avenues of bolt upright figures, with folded arms and all facing alike, and the immense horizontal bases of the pyramids, and the lines of the immense stones which compose them, all illustrate this.

Also, in foundations generally, where permanence is most desirable, the main lines are mostly straight and horizontal.

But in a church, the multitudinous flowing and uptending lines *should* only express the endlessly varied, yet only beautiful and elevated, individual and associated life, that should, visibly, centre in, and flow from the stirring exercises and activities within it.

98. *The circle* is a symbol of monotonous routine, and hence, as a symbol of eternity, represents only a dormant, unprogressive one. It is thus, by reason of its single centre and uniform distance from that to the circumference, and its consequent uniform rate of variation of direction at all points, and its perpetual return to the same point of beginning.

Hence it is peculiarly appropriate that a nation fallen into a state of decay or lethargy, and whose earthly life might then be largely expressed by the stiff, dead straightness of a right line, should adopt the circle as its symbol of eternity, an eternity of endless dull repetitions of *one unvarying round*. "One unvarying round," is just what the circle sensibly is, and it is therefore the natural symbol of a life made up of routine in one unvarying round.

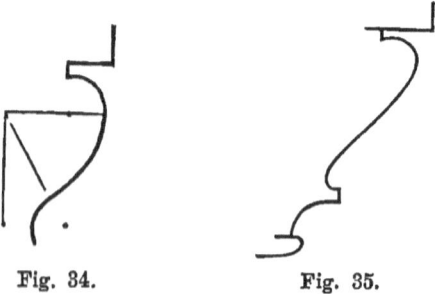

Fig. 34.   Fig. 35.

Again, life is either sensual or spiritual; and, in a given amount of it, as the one prevails, the other is wanting. Now monotony of life indicates absence of thought-activity, and hence, secondarily, the circle as the symbol of monotonous routine, unenlivened by varied thought, is also a symbol of sensuous, more than of intellectual existence. Hence the Romans, who were a grosser, and more materialistic people than the Greeks, spontaneously as it were, made great use of the circle in their architecture, while the Greeks rejected it.

Thus the coarseness of the compound circular moulding, Fig.

34, is apparent in contrast with that of the freely varied principal curve of Fig. 35, whose quick terminal curves, with the more uniform portion, included between them, readily express early entrance upon a prolonged career of excellence, promptly closed where its work is done.

99. The *ellipse* being only the general form, of which the circle is a particular case, it is not expressive of anything radically different from what is symbolized by the circle. Its continually varying rate of curvature expresses more of varied life than the circle does. Also its two foci, representing a two-fold governing purpose, or idea, or all-engaging pursuit, give more of life to it as a symbol.

As contrasted with a circle, for a window, its compression in one direction may make it expressive of partly constrained or contracted, rather than of full-orbed and *equally* all-embracing life and character. Hence elliptical topped windows, for example, are less frequent and pleasing than semi-circular topped ones.

100. Quite otherwise from the foregoing is it with the *hyperbola*, which is sufficiently defined for present purposes by say-

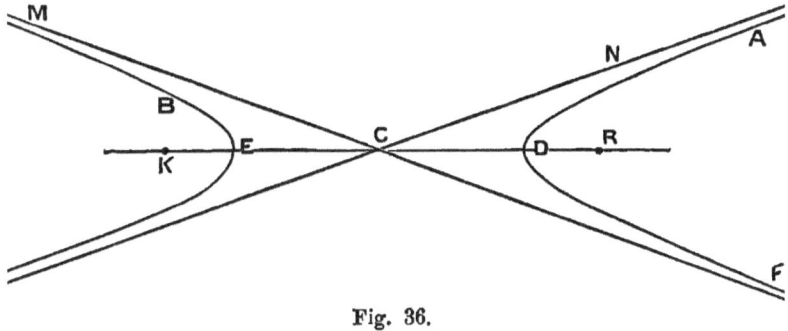

Fig. 36.

ing that it consists of two *equal*, *opposite*, and *infinite* branches, ADF and GEB, Fig. 36, to which a pair of straight lines, M and N, crossing at the centre C, are tangent only at an infinite distance from C. Such lines are called *asymptotes*. The fixed points R and K are called its *foci*, each one, a *focus*.

The complete symbolism of this line is remarkable for its ready and striking truthfulness.

The general idea of the infinite approach of a curve to a straight tangent, as a symbol of an infinite progress towards perfection, or to the absolute ideal, never actually attained, has long been familiar; but is realized in the case of *any* of the many different curves which have asymptotes. The distinctive symbolism of the hyperbola may be more precisely stated.

First, there is *material* civilization, as that of peoples who excel more in material arts, than in personal or national virtues, and there is *moral* civilization, as of peoples or communities eminent for truth, justice, pure patriotism, and philanthropy. Also there is *material* barbarism; and there is *moral* barbarism, illustrated by the injustice or cruelties practised upon weaker, or savage, peoples by nations who were far advanced in many material arts.

Now, in the hyperbola, one asymptote, as M, may represent *material* perfection, or *material* degradation; the former, for example, to the right, and the latter, to the left of C. The other asymptote, N, may then represent to the right of C *moral* perfection, and to the left, its opposite. Thus the two branches of the curve, each tangent to both asymptotes, naturally represent the opposite possibilities of indefinite progress towards good or evil, either material or moral.

101. *Spirals* are, as compared with the circle, noble symbols of immortal life, with growth and progress, inasmuch as, unlike the circle, they do not return into themselves, but ever proceed in wider and wider circuits, expressive of the expansive progress of all noble lives.

They may, therefore, well enter into the composition of the decorative parts, at least, or the seals, or heraldic devices of the buildings whose uses are representative of human progress. And they could hardly appear otherwise than in the ornamental details, because the visible representative of the inspiring idea should be, like the idea itself, over and above the working rooms which must be merely adapted to the work to be done in them.

102. Imagine now a curve, such that the positions of all its points should be governed by one fixed point and one fixed line.

Together with such a curve, imagine any organization, the

various branches, or departments of whose work, should be governed by some one central idea, and some one executive body, representing, so to speak, a certain line of policy.

Such a curve would be a symbol of such an organization; and, if, in future times, attention were paid to symbolism between the inward idea, or purpose, and the outward material agencies through which the idea was put in operation, in all departments of activity, as it has already been in some, nothing would seem more natural than endeavors to realize this symbolism.

103. Thus, for a long time it has been customary to build churches in the form of a cross; to decorate heroes with jewelled, and hence brilliant stars; to mark a court-house (temple of justice) by a statue holding a balance; to crown a building which is the property of a nation, or, in some sense, even of mankind, by a vast dome, expressive of the firmament under which all live.

104. With equal propriety, apparently unthought of only because the field of application is much more recent, might symbolism enter the field of education. It does so on a small scale, when, for instance, a quill is made the device for the vane of a school-house, or an engineering instrument the device used for a breast-pin by the students of a school of engineering, or when the iron fence-posts around a military academy are in the form of cannon, and the pickets in the form of spears. But, on a larger scale, the buildings for the general and special purposes of any large educational establishment, together with the residences for its teaching body, might, if its grounds were sufficiently extensive, be easily arranged in a symbolical manner.

105. Thus, returning now to Art. (102) there are two curves, at least, which agree with the definition there suggested. These are the *parabola*, Fig. 37, each of whose points, as a, is at equal distances, a F and a b, from a *fixed point*, F, the focus, from a *fixed line*, D b, the directrix.

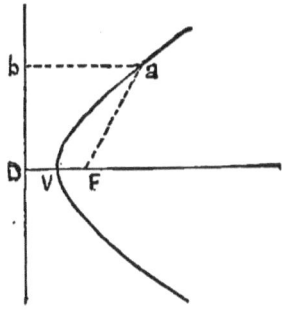

Fig. 37.

Also the *conchoid*, Fig. 38, a curve of two branches, and all of whose points are at the same fixed distance from a *given line*, measured on lines drawn from a *fixed point*. When this point is nearer the fixed line than the fixed distance, one branch of

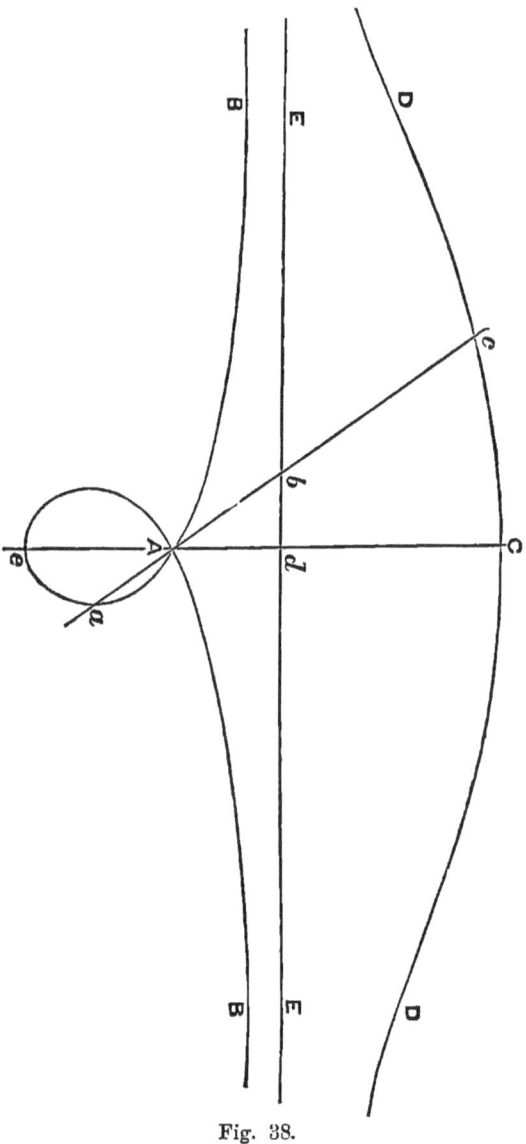

Fig. 38.

the curve will be looped. Thus E E is the fixed line, and A the fixed point. Then $d\,C = d\,e\,;\ \ b\,a = b\,c$, etc.

106. Turning now from these curves to a complex educational establishment, we find for its corresponding fixed elements, 1°, a *foundation course* of *study*, alike for all, 2°, *a teaching* and governing body. There would then be depending upon these (*a*) the various specialties to which the institution might devote itself; (*b*) the incidental features of its life, lodgings, gymnasium, etc.; and finally (*c*) a select group of structures, devoted to the most refined purposes of the institution.

107. *Parabolic plan.* The several elements just stated might find their material organization on a *parabolic plan*, as follows. The collegiate or general building in which the foundation course (1°) should be given, would naturally stand at the focus. The residences of the teaching and governing body (2°) would be located on an avenue marking the directrix. Then, (*a*) the schools for the several specialties or professions, would be arranged at intervals on the curve, and with paths to them located as at F *a* and *b a*. The axis of symmetry, D F, being therefore a special line, and D and V, special points upon it, a chapel, D, library, V, a museum, and observatory may be built upon it.

Subordinate structures might be located at convenience on lines within the curve, and parallel to D F.

108. *The conchoidal plan.* The *conchoid*, when laid out on a grand scale on the ground, permits the *symbolical* expression of the ideas, stated in Art. (106), in the *material* organization of an institution, as its published curriculum exhibits them in the printed expression of the *logical* organization.

1°. A grand building, surmounted with a dome, as the symbol of comprehensiveness, and with lofty porticos facing the four cardinal points of the compass, as the symbol of its equal openness to all, should stand at A, and contain instruction rooms for all the general subjects.

2°. Professors, as the immediate *personal* determining element in the life and work of an institution, should have residences ranged along the fixed determining line E E. And *d e* may be 1000 feet or more.

3°. D D, being the *superior branch* of the curve, should be allotted to the series of buildings devoted to the several professional schools, and reached from A by paths on the radial lines as *a b c*, which determine the points where they stand.

4°. B B, being the inferior branch of the curve, should be devoted to the gymnasium, janitor's lodge, bathing house, lodging, and society buildings.

5°. The loop A e, as a separate and peculiar feature, should be set apart for an elegant enclosure, with fountains, etc., and faced by the observatory, chapel, and library buildings.

109. Education, most comprehensively defined as to its matter, exists in two grand divisions; *humanistic*, or the study of man, his life, and actions; and *naturalistic*, or the study of nature as subservient to man.

If, according to what may be the preference of some, an institution of the most comprehensive or encyclopedic character, embracing both of these grand divisions, were to be planned, its symbolic material organization might best consist in the arrangement of its buildings on the two branches of a hyperbola.

But it is probably better, that, by a proper application in education of the principle of division of labor, only one of these grand divisions of the whole field should be embraced in one institution. If so, there would seem to be no superior to the conchoid for the symbolical ground plan of the buildings collectively, of a great educational establishment of either class.

110. But the *bi-lateral symmetry of the conchoid*, that is, the equality of the halves on each side of the line of symmetry Ce, may be made significant in either of two ways.

First. In case of the adoption of the all-inclusive organization above described, the buildings pertaining to the two grand divisions named, might be arranged; those of the one, on one side, and those of the other, on the other side of Ce.

Second, independently of this, and probably a better symbolic use of this symmetry, would be the following. Each subject of study has its purely scientific side, as related to *truth ;* and its artistic side, as related to *beauty*. Hence, taking, as before, the buildings of but one of the grand divisions described, for distribution on the conchoid plan, the naturalistic one for example; Schools of Industrial Physics, Chemistry, and Engineering could be on one side of Ce, and those of Music, Painting, Architecture, and Decorative Design, on the other.

111. The *positions* of lines have a significance, as well as their forms. Thus a prevalence of *vertical* lines symbolizes as-

piration, upward-tending thought and purpose; and hence gives noble meaning to a lofty gothic cathedral interior, where the prevailing direction of the lines is vertical.

The same idea gives effect to the humblest village spire. Hence the betrayal of offensive vain consciousness, or of obtuseness, either in the maker or beholder, in adding an up-pointing hand to the top of a spire, as if the spire were made to say, "See with what beautiful expressiveness I point to heaven;" or, more likely, as if the mind could not understand the upward pointing of the spire without this explanatory addition, which robs the imagination of its dues in being left free to give meaning to what it sees.

A prevalence of *horizontal* lines, is expressive of a clinging to the earth, as in the popular life of the Greeks, most, or all of whose gods were but exaggerated men, crimes and all; and *then*, set over this world's woods and fields, seas and skies, wars and passions, rather than over a universe of life, to be moulded into enduring forms of living beauty by them. Hence the marked predominance of the horizontal in the Greek temples, with their flat roofs and horizontal mouldings, and flat doors and window tops.

Once more, and in a *derivative* manner, horizontal lines express *firmness, decision, stability*, and hence are the proper characteristic lines of foundations and supports. The repose,

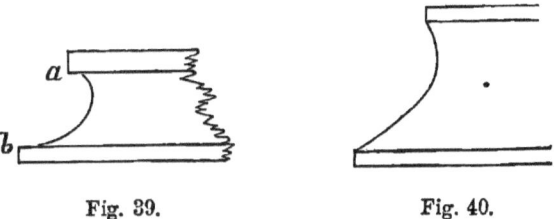

Fig. 39.   Fig. 40.

or fixity, which they primarily signify, leads to the secondary meanings, unchangeableness, and thence decision, or stability, as stated. Hence the curved outlines of mouldings on supporting parts best flow into the horizontal top and bottom surfaces of such parts.

Thus, Figs. 39 and 41, show a better relation of the curved contour, as tangent to the bases, than Fig. 40, does.

112. *Carvings.* Work becomes so costly as soon as straight outlines are abandoned, and especially as carved work begins to be employed, that its consequent difficulty of attainment makes it symbolical of the grace and beauty that can only be had under the best conditions, or, as the result of man's best aspirations; while the plain lines of ordinary work represent,

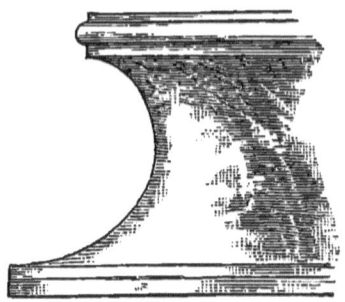

Fig. 41.

by comparison, humbler human industries. Hence a bit of choice carving to crown, or tip, or face a piece of otherwise plain work, happily symbolizes the cheerful co-operation of happiness and honest industry, the meeting of truth and beauty.

It is in the light of such reflections that the *real* vulgarity of mere flat sawed scroll work, on which no elevated intellectual or artistic thought or fond purpose has been exercised, is fully shown. Being purely mechanical products, they can serve no high thought or purpose.

113. *An entirely different principle,* however, governs the employment of ornamental castings from really rich and beautiful designs. Here, the thought is the nobly generous one of bringing to every humble home, by means of a beneficent art of multiplication, beauties of decoration which could not otherwise be had. The "preciousness" of the immediate products of the skilled and refined hand becomes only their hatefulness when they are prized mainly *because* none but one wealthy purchaser can own and enjoy them.

The "ginger-bread" products of the scroll saw, from inch boards, are mean in origin, material, and execution, and are therefore to be discarded for their inherent demerits; but good castings, from beautiful designs, inherit and partake of the characteristics and associations of their original, and are, by all means, to be commended, where originals cannot be had.

Somewhat in the same line of thought with the remarks on carvings; broken pediments, as in the annexed figure, and con-

taining a carved bust or other form of life, may be mentioned as symbolizing the escape of the spirit from the hindrances and imprisonment of the body.

114. Without further illustration, it may now be enough to add that the foregoing somewhat numerous, and widely varied examples may serve to set the thoughts in motion upon the line indicated, so that the student may be aided in his efforts to give to all his works an attractive and elevating *meaning*, at the same time that they fulfil the bare physical conditions required of them.

Apply the principles of this, and the preceding chapters, in designing the following:

Ex. 31. An altar.
Ex. 32. A pulpit.
Ex. 33. A book-case.
Ex. 34. A parlor organ case.
Ex. 36. A church porch.
Ex. 37. A district school-house.
Ex. 38. A sideboard.
Ex. 39. A public library entrance.
Ex. 40. A mantel-piece.

THE END.

www.ingramcontent.com/pod-product-compliance
Lightning Source LLC
Chambersburg PA
CBHW020305170426
43202CB00008B/510